On Board of Bk Mary and Susan

Mr Brown
Mr Rodgers

Larboard
Starboard

35 bbls
30
13
48
35
1.5.3 bbls

8 bbls
10 bbls
58
35
30
20
20 bbls
20 bbls
42 bbls
15
32
_____
289 bbls

13 bbls
55
58 bbls
1.11 bbls
13
13
104
52
35.9½
45 bbls
6
13
_____
5.42 bbls

95 bbls

bbls 35

542
357
247
_____
1185

TRAPPED IN ICE!

This book is for Lila Re Sandler,
who has already filled our
hearts with joy and wonder.

TRAPPED IN ICE!

An Amazing True Whaling Adventure

MARTIN W. SANDLER

SCHOLASTIC NONFICTION

An imprint of

Library of Congress Cataloging-in-Publication Data

Sandler, Martin W.

    Trapped in ice / by Martin Sandler.

       p. cm.

    Includes bibliographical references.

    ISBN 0-439-74363-X

1. Whaling—Arctic regions—History—19th century. I. Title.

SH382.S26 2006

639.2'8'091644—dc22

2005042644

10 9 8 7 6 5 4 3 2 1   06 07 08 09 10

Printed in the U.S.A. 23

First printing, March 2006

Art Direction: Tatiana Sperhacke

Book Design: Kay Petronio

Contents

Introduction

"Never in all man's history," wrote historian Everett S. Allen, "has there ever been anything comparable to whaling in terms of what it demanded of those afloat who pursued it, or the vessels in which they sailed." Allen was right. The challenges faced by the men and boys who, in open boats, pitted themselves against the largest creatures on Earth were more difficult and more dangerous than anything even the most daring souls ever encountered, particularly for those who went whaling in the ice-filled waters of the Far North. The adventures that the whalemen took part in, both in pursuing the whales and sailing throughout the world, rival even the most action-packed fiction.

In 1871, 1,219 men, women, and children sailed to the Arctic in pursuit of the bowhead whale. They hoped to fill their ships with whale oil and bone. But what happened to them was unlike anything that any whaleman in the long history of whaling had ever experienced.

It is a remarkable story, filled with disaster, heroism, unprecedented sacrifice, mystery, and what can only be regarded as miracles. It is even more extraordinary because it really happened.

Martin W. Sandler
Cotuit, Massachusetts

CHAPTER ONE

The Most Dangerous Job in the World

TIS YOUR WHALER alone who goes down to the sea in ships; other mariners hurry across it. He alone does business upon the great waters, and more emphatically than any other "seafarers," makes the ocean his home.

— New England Magazine, *1835*

It was early October 1892. As the tall-masted, canvas-laden whaleship *Helen Mar* made its way through the deep waters of the Arctic, its captain and thirty-eight-man crew were in high spirits. They had had a long and successful voyage. Their ship was almost filled with precious whale oil and bone, and soon they would be returning home to San Francisco. Suddenly, disaster struck.

"On October, 6, when in latitude 71 degrees, 30 minutes north, the vessel took whales," one of the crewmen would later write.

The crew was so busy in [boiling down] the catch that they did not observe the swift current carrying them toward a great ice floe. When they observed their peril there was no time to escape wreck. They got out two [whaleboats] but had no time to get into them before the vessel came in contact with the floe. The sharp edge of the ice cut through the hull as a knife cuts through cheese. In a moment two masts snapped off and fell on the ice and the vessel went down as though the bottom had dropped out.

Just as she was sinking, fifth mate William Ward and four men leaped on the ice floe and saved their lives. They saw the captain and first mate struggling in the water but could not lend any help. In five minutes the captain and 33 men had found a watery grave. The men on the floe besides mate Ward were [harpooner] Anton Pargatino, cook Acy Kershaw, and sailors Koshan and Perores. The situation was very bad, as the floe was swept by icy winds and there was no shelter. They hoisted a shirt on a fragment of spar and waited for help from some passing vessel. They spent 48 hours before their signal was seen by the . . . whaler Orca.

It was a tragedy, but it was far from unique, particularly for men in search of whales in the frozen North. One early whaling captain, upon first taking his ship into Arctic waters, put it this way: "I felt as I gazed upon the great frozen ice fields stretching far down to the horizon that they were barriers placed there by [God] to rebuke our anxious and [all-consuming] pursuit of wealth." He was right. For the Arctic was

Famed New Bedford artist William Bradford titled this painting *Caught in the Floes*, a vivid depiction of the dangers all whalemen faced in the Arctic.

simply the most difficult and most dangerous place to pursue whales.

A land of ice, snow, fog, and vicious storms, the Arctic is marked by the constant changes in weather that take place, commonly within a single day, often within a single hour. On any given day in the winter and early spring, temperatures may range from thirty-five degrees below zero to fourteen degrees above. The average winter temperature is thirty below. Adding to the bitter temperatures are the constant Arctic winds ceaselessly churning up the waters, driving huge waves ashore.

Even more threatening to Arctic mariners than the howling winds are the long periods of fog, often so thick that navigating in the already treacherous waters becomes virtually impossible. "Fogs are frequent and dense," wrote whaling historian Alexander Starbuck. "It frequently happens that the crew of [a whaleboat] will fail to find their own ship and will meet with some other; in which case they have no hesitation in [climbing] aboard the stranger, there to remain until the fog lifts and they can find their own vessel."

But even more than the ever-changing conditions, the life-threatening temperatures, the fog, and the constant winds, the greatest peril faced by those who went whaling in the Arctic was the continual threat of having their ships crushed in the ice. Beginning in the early fall, enormous masses of ice form, signaling what, by winter, will be the transformation of the frigid waters into an often unbroken expanse of ice that will remain until early summer or even later. Lagoons and other sheltered bodies of water become locked in ice more than two feet thick.

For mariners, particularly whalemen already engaged in one of the world's most hazardous undertakings, the Arctic ice presented the greatest challenge most would ever face. As the unfortunate souls of the *Helen Mar* discovered all too well, contact with a single knife-edged ice pack could send even the sturdiest whaleship to the bottom within minutes. Avoiding the drifting or, worse yet, wind-driven ice tested both the navigational skills and courage of even the most experienced whaling captain. No wonder that more whaleships were destroyed by ice than by all other causes combined.

Given the hardships and dangers, it may seem surprising that, in the last half of the 1800s, thousands of American men signed on for whaling voyages to the Arctic. Actually, they were hardly all men. More than half the members of a whaleship crew were typically boys

"The Roving Whalers"

———— ◎ ————

AS THEY RELENTLESSLY PURSUED THE BOWHEAD through far northern regions where few others had ever journeyed, American whalemen made a vital contribution that went beyond their supplying people everywhere with products from the whale. By continually sailing into the unknown or the uncharted they became practically the only explorers of the Arctic Ocean, and at least half of all polar discovery was made by them.

For whalemen, this type of discovery was nothing new. As author Richard Ellis reminds us, "In their search for oil [and whalebone] the roving whalers opened the world, much as the explorers of the 16th century had done in their quest for the riches of the Indies."

American whalemen were among the first to sail around Cape Horn and enter the South Pacific Ocean. They were the first to sail into Japanese ports and were instrumental in opening up that long-isolated nation to foreigners. As they pursued the whale from Africa to Brazil, from Chile to Japan, from pole to pole, they discovered more than four hundred islands, giving many of them American names. And it was the whalers who gave the world the first chart of the Gulf Stream, and who unlocked many of the ages-old secrets of currents and tides — all while chasing whales.

under the age of nineteen. So, why did they do it? Why did they risk their lives to hunt the largest creatures on Earth? There were almost as many reasons as there were those who shipped aboard.

Many who took up whaling were men who were out of work, desperate for any employment they could find. Others were young men from rural areas, tired of farmwork, eagerly seeking the adventure of traveling the world and of pursuing and capturing the mammoth and always dangerous whales. Still others had been recruited by agents hired by whaleship owners, men who would falsely promise a would-be whaler almost anything in order to get him to sign aboard. "He told me fine stories about how much money I would make and what a pleasant voyage I would have," one young country lad recalled. "None of it was true."

Along with the desire for adventure, the most compelling reason that whalemen had for pursuing the whales was the glory they felt they would attain. Young Peter Dumont made his first whaling voyage aboard the *Mammoth*. Later he reminisced about why he went. "Whaling," Dumont stated, "is about as hazardous and dangerous an occupation as any to which we could have devoted ourselves, but this idea never occurred to our minds, so engrossed were we by reflections on the glories and advantages we hoped to reap before our return." Among the advantages that young Dumont might have had in mind was success with the young ladies. For it was well known throughout whaling ports like New Bedford and Nantucket, Massachusetts, that among the men who went courting in those whaling centers, those who had the best chance with the prettiest girls were the ones who could honestly boast that they had killed a whale.

Yet no matter how strong their reasons for going, there were always doubts, particularly if, as was the case with young Nelson Cole Haley, it was their first whaling voyage. "It went through my mind, why should I cause myself such sad feelings by taking this voyage?" Haley confided to his diary shortly after his ship put out to sea. "Here I was, leaving home perhaps never to return and for no satisfactory reason I could give; leaving behind a happy home and friends who had done what they could to have me stay home with them. I knew what I had to face, that at least was sure: storms, gales, hurricanes . . . and whales' jaws and flukes. For what? Not for money. Because not much of that comes to the crew. Well, it might be for the wish to command a ship, in proper time. Still, was it worth it?"

Haley might have wondered if whaling was worth it, but the men who owned the whaleships had no doubt. Throughout the 1800s whaling was, for the owners and for the captains of their vessels who were well paid, one of the most profitable of all enterprises. It was an extremely important endeavor as well. Up until the late 1860s, the main prey of most whalemen was the sperm whale, which traveled through warm waters throughout the globe. In an age before electricity, the huge amounts of oil extracted from sperm whales provided the world with the finest of all fuel used to light the lamps of the day. Sperm oil was also used to make candles and to lubricate almost every type of machine.

For decades it appeared that the passion for hunting the sperm whale would never end. "Where would we be without the whalemen?" a newspaper editor wrote. "Their hard and greasy work gives us light and runs our machines. Our indebtedness to them knows no bounds." It was an opinion with which few could disagree. But America in the last half of the nineteenth century was a nation in which new advancements and new discoveries were being made one after another. One of the most important of these took place in 1859 when oil was found deep underneath the ground in

Titusville, Pennsylvania. Soon vast, rich deposits of oil were discovered in other places. It would take more than a decade to develop the know-how and the equipment necessary to extract and refine oil efficiently, but by the late 1860s oil from beneath the land was being extracted and purified in such enormous quantities that the demand for whale oil dropped as sharply as it had first arisen. The glory days of hunting the sperm whale were coming to an end.

But aside from oil, there was another important product extracted from whales. It was whalebone, out of which were made scores of goods that were a vital part of nineteenth-century life. In a time long before plastics and flexible steel, a time when people commonly moved about on horseback or in horse-drawn vehicles, whalebone was used to make buggy whips, riding crops, and carriage springs. Other products made from whalebone included clothespins, umbrella ribs, shoehorns, canes, pie cutters, fishing poles, and hoops for ladies' skirts. In an age when almost all women wore painfully tight corsets to make them appear as slim as possible, strips of whalebone called stays, which enabled corsets to retain their shape, became the most commonly used whalebone product of all.

Details from a nineteenth-century lithograph illustrate how people benefited from the products derived from the whale, including lamp oil, candles, food, umbrella and corset stays, fertilizer, and oil for lubricating machinery.

THE WHALE

SHOWING THEIR UTILITY TO MAN, IN THEIR EMPLOYMENTS
DURING LIFE & USES AFTER DEATH.

As the value of whale oil decreased, whalebone, because of its many uses, actually gained in value, and by the late 1860s, whalemen's attention turned away from the sperms to a different type of whale, one whose body contained more bone than any other species. It was the bowhead, and it was a remarkable creature. Instead of teeth, a bowhead had hundreds of bone slabs called baleen, many of which were more than twelve feet long. Bent in an arc inside the bowhead's huge bow-shaped mouth, these slabs were used as strainers for capturing the shrimplike crustaceans, jellyfish, and other tiny marine animals upon which this whale fed. From the time in 1848 when whaling captain Thomas Roys sailed into the Arctic's Bering Sea and had introduced American whalemen to the bowhead, the amount of bone that could be taken from certain of these whales became legendary.

In 1859 the crew of the *Northern Light* made headlines by killing and processing a bowhead that yielded 3,181 pounds of bone. The crew of another vessel harpooned and stripped down a bowhead whose gigantic mouth contained 620 slabs of bone. But even these creatures paled in comparison to the bowhead captured by Captain Bony Rice in the Arctic in 1851. After the slabs from the mouth of this monstrous whale were extracted, washed, and dried, they weighed more than five thousand pounds, worth more than $200,000 in today's money.

What Bony Rice and other early American whaling captains who followed him into the Arctic quickly learned was that, aside from their enormous amounts of bone, there were other ways in which bowheads differed from the sperm whales that whalers had previously pursued. They discovered, for example, that in some ways bowheads were easier to hunt. Because they were slow, leisurely swimmers, bowheads most often could be approached in a whaleboat without difficulty. And, unlike the sperm whales, they were not fierce fighters and had no teeth or powerful jaws to use to attack the boats.

All this did not mean that capturing bowheads was simple and without real danger. Far from it. While they had no viselike jaws, bowheads had extremely powerful flukes (tail lobes), which could shatter a whaleboat. Like the sperm whales, bowheads were immense creatures, possessed with great strength, speed, and endurance. Early pursuers of these whales were astounded to find that in some instances a bowhead they had harpooned immediately descended straight down into the ocean for nearly a mile. Other whalers were similarly shocked when they discovered that some of the bowheads they harpooned took off away from them at speeds of up to twenty-five miles an hour. The log of the early-nineteenth-century whaleship *Resolution* recorded an instance in which a bowhead that the crew of one of the ship's whaleboats had harpooned was finally killed after a chase of more than nine miles.

The greatest challenge of all in hunting bowheads, however, had to do with where they lived. When a bowhead was harpooned, its instincts took over and it immediately headed for the nearest ice pack, knowing that if it could get underneath, it would be safe. The trick in hunting a bowhead was to get right on top of the whale, harpoon it, and kill it before it was lost under the ice.

In 1846 whaleman John Ross Browne wrote a book describing his first whaling voyage. In it he recalled the words that an agent had used to lure him into his whaling trip. "Whaling . . . ," the agent had said, "is tolerably hard at first, but it's the finest business in the world for enterprising young men. . . . Vigilance and activity will insure your rapid promotion. . . . A whaler is a place of refuge for the distressed . . . there's nothing like it. You can see the world; you can see something of life!"

Twenty-five years after the agent uttered these words, 39 ships and 1,219 people prepared to set sail for the Arctic, intent on filling their vessels with bone from the bowhead whale. The agent's words, spoken a quarter century before, would prove prophetic. Those aboard the vessels would indeed see "something of life." But it would be more than any of them would ever have wished to have witnessed.

S. Thomas & Co., corner Front and Union Streets, New Bedford.

Sperm and Whale Oil, Sperm Candles, Sperm and Whale Oil Soap.

The text that accompanied this drawing, which appeared on the stationery of a New Bedford waterfront store, informed customers of the several products from the sperm whale that the store offered for sale.

CHAPTER TWO

Preparing for Adventure

THEY HUNTED WHALES for lubricant,

Those hardy men in little ships,

For oil for lamps, perfumes and canes,

For corset stays and buggy whips.

— *Whalers' song, ca. 1850*

As the 1871 Arctic whaling season approached, some of the world's finest whaling vessels gathered in Honolulu, Hawaii, a popular port from which to sail to far northern waters. Twenty-two of the ships that would make up the thirty-nine-vessel fleet were from New Bedford, Massachusetts, the world's greatest whaling port. Others were from San Francisco; New London, Connecticut; Edgartown, Massachusetts; and Honolulu itself. A few ships of the fleet had chosen to sail directly from their home ports and would join up with the others in the Arctic.

The typical whaling voyage began with the captain calling all hands on deck once the ship was out of sight of land. Then he would look directly at the crew and address them with words like these: "This is a whaleship. We're out to kill whales. I'm the captain and these are my officers and when an order is given you're to obey it immediately. Loafing and grumbling will not be allowed. If any of you want trouble, you can be sure that I will see that you get it. The sooner you fill this ship with whale oil the sooner you'll get home. Now jump to it."

If his words seemed harsh, they were absolutely necessary, for maintaining discipline in order to assure the efficiency of the crew and the safety of the ship was but one of the captain's responsibilities. There were many others. It was the captain's duty to oversee the onboard training of the raw youngsters who made up a large portion of any whaling crew and, before the long voyage was over, to make men out of boys.

Although almost no whaling captains had any medical training, they also had to fulfill the role of ship's doctor to men engaged in the most dangerous type of work. With only their experience and a medical book to guide them, they extracted infected teeth, set broken bones, and, when necessary, even performed amputations. And when punishment was called for, it was up to the captain to decide whether a crewman's transgression was serious enough for him to be flogged or put in irons.

When whales were sighted, the captain took on a whole new set of responsibilities. It was he who commanded the pursuit and capture of the whales, often jumping into a whaleboat to personally take part in the action. He also oversaw all the onboard processing once the whales were brought back to the ship.

Demanding as these responsibilities were, most captains were equal to the task. Almost all were seasoned seamen who had risen up through the whaling ranks. Captain Joseph Homes, for example, was thirteen years

RIGHT: Along with his many other responsibilities, every whaling captain served as the navigator of his vessel, a task that was even more difficult if his ship was headed for ice-filled Arctic waters.

old when he first worked on a whaleship, was sixteen when he served as a mate on another vessel, and became a captain when he was twenty-one.

Whatever age he was, by the time a whaleman became captain, he had seen it all and had learned to take every aspect of whaling in stride, including that of being away from home for years at a time. One of the favorite stories that made the rounds of the seaport taverns where mariners gathered was that of the whaling captain who had forgotten to kiss his wife before his ship departed. When criticized for this lack of devotion, he reportedly replied, "Well, we expected to be gone for only two years."

Disciplinarians, teachers, navigators, doctors, morale boosters, whalemen — the captains were all of these and more. They would never have succeeded if they had not possessed yet another essential trait: their confidence in meeting their greatest responsibility of all, that of returning home with every available space in the ship filled with barrels of oil and whalebone.

"This is the first voyage that I ever took charge of," Captain Henry Green confided to his diary. "I am very young at the business and my ship is very old. I am 26 1/2 years old. The ship is 79. I have but two men before the mast that have ever been more than one voyage at sea. [But] if there are any whales living, we will get [them]."

A whaling vessel that returned to port with less than a full cargo of oil was referred to as having made a "brokcn voyage," something that every man in charge of a whaleship regarded as the ultimate disgrace. "If I live to reach home," stated the logbook of Captain Leonard Gifford, "no man shall be able to say to me, 'there goes a fellow that brought home a broken voyage.'"

Among the men who commanded the whaleships preparing to leave Honolulu was Connecticut-born Horace Newbury, who was looking forward to repeating the Arctic whaling adventure he had experienced a decade earlier. Like thousands of other boys who had grown up along the New England coast, Newbury had developed a yearning for the sea when he was still a child. He was only twelve years old when he got his first seafaring job, as a cook on a fishing vessel. By the time he was twenty, he had become a mate on a whaling ship that, in 1860, had challenged the Arctic waters in search of bowheads.

By 1864, Newbury had risen to the rank of captain, and over the next seven years commanded two different whaleships that made successful Arctic voyages.

New Bedford

──── ◉ ────

"IN NEW BEDFORD," exclaimed famed American author and philosopher Ralph Waldo Emerson, "they hug an oil cask like a brother." It was true. Throughout the last half of the 1800s, New Bedford was the whaling center of the world, with more whaleships sailing out of that city than from all the other whaling ports of the world combined.

The most visible evidence of New Bedford's whaling predominance was the city itself. The cobblestone streets running down to its harbor were among the busiest in the nation. All along them were housed shipowners' and merchants' offices, banks, and maritime insurance companies. There also were scores of nautical supply establishments, seamen's clothing stores, carpenters' shops, and spacious buildings known as sail lofts, where huge pieces of canvas were spread out, measured, cut, and stitched into the sails that powered New Bedford's whaling fleet. Among the busiest of the establishments were the dozens of blacksmiths' shops where harpoons, lances, ship fittings, anchors, and other essential whaling supplies were fashioned. Here too were the bustling shipyards, where whaleships were built and repaired, and long buildings where miles of rope, so essential to the whaleman's trade, were manufactured.

It was a unique and wealthy place, accentuated by the scores of imposing mansions owned by whaling merchants and whaleship owners, and there was no doubt about what had made it so. "Whence came all the wealth?" exclaimed author Herman Melville. "It was harpooned and dragged up from the bottom of the sea."

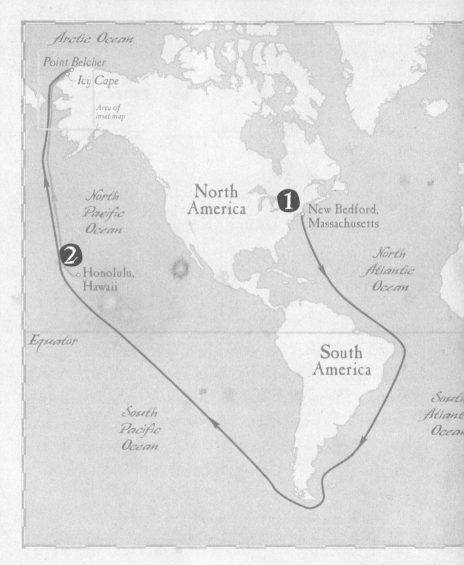

This map shows the route taken by those ships of the 1871 fleet that left New Bedford, Massachusetts ❶ and sailed to the whaling grounds off Point Belcher ❸, a voyage of some 16,500 miles. It also shows the route to Point Belcher taken by the ships that departed from Honolulu, Hawaii ❷, a trip of nearly 2,200 miles.

Also shown is the 80-mile route down the narrow channel from Point Belcher to Icy Cape **4** that the 1,219 imperiled whalemen and their wives and children took in search of rescue.

Included among his experiences as a whaling master were the several medical operations he had performed at sea, the rescue of the crew of a sinking ship, and the time he had been forced to stay on his feet armed with two pistols for almost two weeks, with little sleep, in order to prevent a mutiny from taking place aboard his ship.

Like Horace Newbury, the *J. D. Thomson*'s captain, Charles Allen was also eagerly awaiting the day when the carpenters, riggers, warehousemen, and other craftsmen and suppliers would finish making the fleet ready to sail. On one of his previous excursions into northern waters, Allen had returned with one of the most profitable cargoes of bone and oil ever harvested from the sea.

As he strode the deck of the *Champion*, Captain Henry Pease was probably not as excited about the impending voyage as was Charles Allen. Pease knew all too well what could lie ahead of him and his crew. Only a year earlier he had returned from the Arctic after enduring one of the most harrowing experiences of his life at sea.

"On the evening of [October] 7th," he had written in his journal, "it blew almost a hurricane; hove the ship to south of Point Hope, with the main-topsail furled; lost starboard bow [whaleboat]. On the tenth, the heaviest sea I ever saw; . . . ship covered with ice and oil . . . no fire to cook with or to warm by, made it the most anxious and miserable time I ever experienced in all my sea service. . . . At daylight on the second day . . . the gale moderated a little . . . had it not moderated as soon as it did, we should by 10 A.M. have been shaking hands with our departed friends."

Captain Thomas Williams on the *Monticello* had also had more than his share of whaling experiences in general and Arctic adventures in particular. He was not only arguably the most experienced of all the masters of the fleet, but he was also the head of one of whaling's most remarkable families.

During his many years of command, Williams had earned the respect of almost all who sailed with him, including his son William Fish Williams, who served under him on two whaling voyages. "I had an intense respect for my father; he has always been to me the finest type of man I have ever known," William would later write. "He stood six feet three inches in his stocking feet, was broad-shouldered, straight as an arrow, blue eyes, large and fine-shaped head, and weighed two hundred pounds with no superfluous flesh. He was a natural leader and commander of men, being utterly fearless but not reckless, and a thorough master of his profession. Like

most men who follow an outdoor life, of a more or less hazardous nature, he was reserved. He was always ready to enforce an order by physical means, if necessary, but he was not a bully or a boaster."

Despite the pleas of his mother, Thomas Williams had run away from home while still a youngster and had shipped aboard a New Bedford whaleship. The courage and skill he displayed on that voyage became known in New Bedford, and on his next two whaling trips he served as a harpooner. When these voyages were completed, he signed on as a mate on a journey that took him on a search for whales halfway around the world.

In 1851 he assumed his first command of a whaleship, and between that year and 1868 he made eight voyages to whaling grounds around the globe. More than most of his fellow captains of the 1871 fleet, Williams knew what challenges lay ahead of him in the Arctic. Only a year before taking command of the *Monticello*, his vessel *Hibernia* had been struck by an ice floe and destroyed.

Unlike most of his fellow captains, Thomas Williams knew that he would have the comfort and assistance of his wife on the Arctic voyage. A woman well ahead of her

LEFT: Throughout the last half of the 1800s, New Bedford, Massachusetts, with its canvas-laden ships and the hundreds of oil-filled barrels lining its docks, was the whaling capital of the world.

time, Eliza Azelia Williams preferred to accompany her husband on some of his adventures rather than spend months or even years at home waiting for his return. Her son William would later write that she "was a little woman, weighing less than one hundred pounds, and could stand erect under my father's outstretched arm without touching it. But when a situation arose that called for the kind of courage that sweeps away all evidence of fear and leaves the mind in calm control, she was superb." William would always remember in particular the time when a crewman on one of his father's vessels suffered a horrendous face wound after a gun exploded aboard ship. After several of the strongest whalemen grew faint attempting to hold the mutilated man's head up while the captain applied scores of stitches, Eliza Williams took over and, according to her son, "finished the job."

Eliza was five months pregnant the first time that she accompanied her husband on a whaling trip, which kept them at sea more than three years. Prior to the departure of the 1871 fleet, she had already taken part in five whaling journeys and had given birth to three of her children while sailing in distant waters. She had been aboard the *Hibernia* when it was sunk by ice, and the courage she displayed during that ordeal had earned her the admiration of every member of her husband's crew.

She was also an intensely curious person, particularly fascinated with every aspect of whaling. The journal she kept aboard her husband's vessel during her first long whaling adventure (from 1858 to 1861) provides more insight into the whaling process than most of the captains' or mates' logbooks that were ever completed. Her journal entry for August 13, 1861, for example, reads: "It has been a fine day and a good breeze. This morning . . . we got one whale . . . we have got him cut in now. It was a bad and long job for the whale was bloated so bad by laying so long. There is quite an offensive odor to that I don't fancy much. That odor with the smoke . . . from the tryworks is quite unpleasant, but I can bear it all first rate when I consider it is filling our ship all the time and by and by it will all be over and we will go home. We have lost some of the head, not leaving it on deck, and the gum that holds the bone was loose and tender and the heft of the bone caused it to give way and it went overboard and sank. It is a very fat whale, the oil is running in streams."

Early in her first voyage Eliza Williams's curiosity about all things having to do with whaling led to her having an experience that probably no other woman ever had. Her journal entry for December 14, 1858, stated: "This morning the men were up as soon as they could see to work, cutting in the whale. It had rained very hard all night and all the morning it had come down in torrents. The poor men had a bad time, all of them wet to their skins. I went up on deck while they were hoisting the head up. It certainly is a great curiosity. My husband wanted me to walk in the whale's mouth. He pushed me up . . . so I can say that I have been inside a whale's mouth. Six or eight people could easily go in and sit down at one time. I would not hesitate . . . sitting down if it was clean, but it was very wet and dirty from the rain."

Eliza Williams's first voyage on one of her husband's whaleships had taken them through the Indian and Pacific oceans and then north to where she had her first encounter with the bowhead whale. In her journal she described that special feature of the bowhead that, although she could not have known it at the time, would lead to the voyage upon which she and the rest of the fleet would embark in 1871. "One cannot imagine without seeing it, how the mouth [of the bowhead] looks," she wrote. "Those long slabs of bone, set as thick together in the jaw as they can be — two rows of them — are like two rows of teeth though nothing like them in looks. I should say that the longest of these slabs was about six feet, but they tell me it is not at all uncommon to see them 15 or 20 feet long. These grow gradually shorter all the way from the back of the head to the entrance of the mouth, being quite short there — not more than two or three inches — and the hair very thick and white. All the rest, the whole length of the slabs, have hair on the edge, making the whole mouth lined with hair. . . . I could not imagine for what purpose this hair was, till my Husband explained it to me. It seems that their food floats in masses, literally covering the water in spots. It is a fine substance, about as big as mustard seed, and surrounded by a gluey substance. This food floats on top of the water. The whale moves along with his mouth open and draws in large quantities of it and it is strained through this hair. It seems singular that such fine food should have been formed for so large a fish. These fish are truly one of the wonderful works of God and well may we think that everything in the deep is wonderful."

Also aboard the *Monticello* as it prepared to set sail were three of Thomas and Eliza Williams's children: Stancel, William, and Mary. Born on the whaleship *Florida*, Stancel was the couple's oldest child. His father

Women at Sea

---- ◉ ----

ELIZA AZELIA WILLIAMS was far from alone in accompanying her husband on a whaling voyage. Whaleship owners dictated that only their captains' wives could join the men at sea, and over the years hundreds of captains' wives sailed aboard whaling vessels. Like Eliza Williams, some of these women were truly fascinated with all that went on in whaling. "It is truly wonderful to me," wrote Mary Lawrence, whose husband captained the vessel *Addison*, "the whole process from the taking of the [fearsome] . . . monster of the deep 'til the oil is in the casks. I want to see everything that is going on. I may never have another opportunity."

Most of these wives joined their husbands at sea to provide comfort to them and to ease their own loneliness. A number of them, however, contributed much more. One captain's wife, Mrs. Nathaniel Jernagen, risked her life to put out a serious fire that broke out on her husband's vessel. Mrs. Charles Grant earned the gratitude of her husband's crew when one day, while hanging out the wash, she spotted the spout of a giant whale that the lookouts had missed. Her cry of "there she blows" galvanized the crew into action. After the creature was killed and boiled down, it yielded more oil than almost any other whale captured on the entire voyage.

The honor of being the most heroic of captain's wives belongs perhaps to Caroline Mayhew, whose husband skippered the whaleship *Powhatan*. When, in 1846, the often fatal disease called smallpox spread through the *Powhatan*, striking down Captain Mayhew and eight members of his crew, Caroline worked night and day and eventually nursed the desperately ill men back to health. During the time her husband was critically ill, Mrs. Mayhew even took over the job of navigating the ship. In gratitude for all she had done, the crew of the *Powhatan* presented her with gifts that they had carved out of whalebone.

was determined that his firstborn not enter the dangerous world of whaling, and at a young age Stancel was sent off to private school. However, he had obviously inherited both of his parents' love of adventure and now, eighteen years old, he had persuaded his father to sign him on as one of the *Monticello*'s mates for the upcoming voyage.

Eleven-year-old William Fish Williams had also been born on his father's ship *Florida*. His three-year journey on that vessel had imbued him with both a love of the sea and a yearning to see as much of the world as he could. Although he too had suffered through the sinking of the *Hibernia*, his desire to return to the Arctic had not diminished, and he was happily looking forward to serving as the *Monticello*'s cabin boy.

The youngest member of this remarkable whaling family was Stancel's and William's sister, Mary. Only nine years old, she had spent almost her entire life on a whaleship. The courage she had displayed when the *Hibernia* was crushed by ice made her parents confident that she would be able to withstand whatever this latest venture into the Arctic had to offer.

Among the captains already at sea and headed for the Arctic was Thomas Williams's brother Lewis. Like Thomas, Lewis had ignored his parents' wishes and had gone to sea at an early age, sailing as a seaman on one of his brother's whaleships. Over the next decade he made several voyages, rising in the ranks from boatsteerer to mate. The *Fanny*, which he was taking to join up with the other vessels of the 1871 fleet, was the first ship to be placed under his command. Accompanying him was his wife who, like her sister-in-law Eliza, was eagerly anticipating being part of her husband's Arctic undertaking.

When Lewis Williams's vessel *Fanny* had left New Bedford to head for the Arctic, and when the other

Whaleships were not as sleek as many other types of sailing vessels, but with their tall masts, billowing sails, and finely crafted whaleboats mounted on their sides, they were often an imposing sight, particularly when first sailing out of port.

twenty-one members of the fleet from that port had set sail for Honolulu to be outfitted, the city's waterfront area had come alive. All along the docks, hundreds of relatives, friends, and townspeople stood watching as the vessels put out to sea. Scores of others watched the departure from railing-enclosed platforms called "walks" (later known as "widow's walks") on the roofs of houses that overlooked the harbor. Many of the onlookers were gaily waving good-bye. Others had more somber expressions, knowing how long the whalers would be gone, realizing that the return of any whaleship was uncertain.

When the day finally arrived for the ships in Honolulu Harbor to get under way, the same type of departure scene was repeated. Once again, hundreds of onlookers bid farewell to the ships and their crews. Many of those aboard the vessels, however, were too taken up with their own thoughts to respond to the well-wishers. Many had heard too many stories about what had befallen other ships and other mariners in their quest for the precious whalebone. Some, like Thomas Williams and his family, had experienced these misadventures firsthand. All could not help wondering what lay ahead for them. One thing, they knew, was for certain: They would soon find out.

CHAPTER THREE

Thar She Blows

DID YOU EVER HEAR tell of

that mighty whale

That when boldly attacked in his lair,

With one sweep of his

mighty and ponderous tail

Sends the whaleboat so high in the air?

— *Whalers' song, ca. 1860*

"No man," wrote Herman Melville in his classic whaling novel, *Moby Dick*, "can feel stronger emotions than that man does, who for the first time finds himself pulling into the charmed, churned circle of the hunted sperm whale." Melville was speaking of all those who went in search of the giant sperms, but he might as well have been referring specifically to the men of the 1871 fleet, particularly the green hands, the raw youngsters who were embarking upon their first whaling voyage.

By leaving Honolulu in January, the masters of the various ships allowed themselves ample time to reach the Arctic well after winter conditions had left that region. They were confident that by the time they arrived, it would be safe to hunt the bowheads. En route to the Arctic they would pass through the much warmer waters that were the home of the great sperm whale. And while bone from the bowhead was their main objective, filling their barrels with oil extracted from the sperms was important to them as well. Aside from the profits that whale oil could still bring them, the captains had another reason for hunting the sperms. Before reaching the Arctic, they needed to make whalemen out of the new sailors, or green hands, who, on many of the vessels, made up at least half the crew.

The training of the green hands would take place from dawn to dark all the way to the Arctic. And it would begin by teaching the novices how to pull at the oars of the long, sleek whaleboats in which they would pursue their prey. Over and over again, the boats were lowered as the green hands were drilled in the art of handling the long, cumbersome oars in unison with their fellow rowers. Many had never been in a boat, let alone gone whaling, and their initial efforts would have been humorous if it was not such a deadly serious business, one on which their lives could very well depend.

The pursuit of the whales, the green hands soon learned, began with a sudden shout from, as it seemed to them, out of the heavens. High in the masts lookouts bellowed, "Thar she blows," or "She blows," or any one of a dozen other shrill exclamations indicating that whales had been spotted. Immediately two other cries were heard, these from the captain. "Stand by to lower the boats," he bellowed, followed by, "Lower away."

Six men took their places in each of the whaleboats, the boatheader at the rear, steering each vessel, the harpooner at the forward oar. Only the boatheader faced forward; the rest rowed with their backs toward whatever lay ahead. For the green hands, it was their most frightening experience thus far. It was scary enough to be after their first whale, but to be rowing toward the creature without being able to see it was nothing short of terrifying.

Aware of their potential panic, the boatheader goaded them on. "Pull, men," he shouted. "Pull as you've never pulled before. Bend your backs. We're gaining. That whale is ours, I tell ye. Oh boys, if you could see that whale. That whale will shorten our voyage by six months.

The long strips of toothlike bone called baleen contained in the cavernous mouth of the bowhead were the main prize sought by those who went whaling in the Arctic.

Why the Harry don't you pull? Oh boys, if you want to see your sweethearts, you'll pull ahead. I'll give ye tobacco. I'll give ye rum. I'll give ye anything if you'll only pull."

Then, as abruptly as he had been shouting, the boatheader began to talk softly, a sure sign that they were close to the whale. "Steady, lads," he whispered. "Steady, steady." The sudden change in tone was necessary, for the whale's acute sense of hearing made it essential to approach him as quietly as possible. One splash of an oar could scare the creature, causing it to dive out of sight or to swim miles away from the boat. Now the harpooner stood up, ready to dart his "iron" as soon as he was a few feet from the whale.

The moment of truth had come, one eloquently described by early whaling chronicler Arthur Watson. "Everything," Watson explained, "depended upon that opening moment. The boat had crept up to its unwitting, peaceful quarry. Nearer and nearer — sliding up to the animal to keep out of his limited vision — close to those dangerous [jaws] — a matter of a few feet only — wood to black skin! That was a moment when nerve and skill were taxed to their utmost, for it was the zero hour. The men had yet to be intoxicated and emboldened by the panic and noise of the drag. The harpoon whizzed. What if it had missed? Well, a boat's crew would have been spared a little taste of pandemonium, but the taverns would not have welcomed them upon their homecoming, and, besides, one of New Bedford's palatial mansions might never have been built."

Harpooning a whale was one thing; killing it was yet something else again. The harpooned whale would often immediately dive deep beneath the surface. When this happened, the men in the boat put up their oars, waiting for the whale to reappear. Maddened by the harpoon within him and the tension of the line to which it was secured, the whale often resurfaced in a fury, sometimes leaping out of the water. This diving and resurfacing could be repeated several times, and the whaling annals were filled with stories of boats that were shattered and whalemen who were killed when one of the whales either came up directly underneath their vessel or landed directly on top of it.

If a harpooned whale did not dive, it most often simply took off on a mad flight, pulling the boat after it at speeds of up to twenty miles per hour. "The whale started off to windward with us at a tremendous rate," first-time whaleman Frank Bullen confided to his journal. "The speed at which he went made it seem as if a gale was blowing, and we flew along the sea surface, leaping from crest to crest of the waves. . . . The flying spray drenched us and prevented us from seeing him."

Whether the secured whale dove beneath the waters or took the whalemen off for what could be miles on what they called a "Nantucket sleigh ride," the purpose was to stay with him until he became so exhausted that the boat could once again draw up next to him and he could be killed by driving a long, razor-sharp lance into his lungs.

"The whale now ran," wrote whaleman Henry Cheever, "and took the line out of the boat with such swiftness that we were obliged to throw water on it to prevent its taking fire by friction around the loggerhead. Then he stopped and blindly thrashed and rolled about in great agony, so that it seemed madness to approach him. By this time, however, the captain came up and boldly darted another harpoon into his writhing body. The enraged whale raised his head above the water, snapped his horrid jaws together, and in his senseless fury lashed the sea into foam with his flukes. The mate now, in his turn, approached near enough to bury a lance deep into his vitals, and shouted at the top of his voice, 'stern all.' A thick stream of blood, instead of water, was soon issuing from his spout holes. Another lance was buried;

The Harpoon

THERE HAS ALWAYS BEEN some question as to who were the first to use harpoons in capturing whales. Some whaling experts claim that it was the Basques who, as early as A.D. 900, hunted the creatures in northern waters. It was the Basques who gave the weapon its name, calling it an *arpoi*, which in English means "harpoon" or "harpooning iron." Other students of whaling claim that the ivory and bone instruments employed by the earliest ancestors of the Eskimos, also called Inuits, were the first to be used. Whoever was first, one thing is for certain: The harpoon was the whaleman's most indispensable weapon.

Over the years many whalemen described the harpoon in the journals they kept, none more accurately than John Ross Browne. "First in importance is the harpoon," Browne wrote. "This instrument, called in whaling parlance, an 'iron,' is generally between three or four feet long, with a bearded head and a shaft or handle of hickory, oak, or dog-wood. . . . In ordinary cases, only one harpoon is made use of [in latching onto a whale] but should it [fall out] or the whale prove difficult to manage, it is not unusual to dart three or four."

Browne used the word *dart* loosely because, contrary to popular belief, the harpoon was not light or javelin-like. Rather, it was a heavy and clumsy implement, which could not be thrown more than fifteen or twenty feet.

There were many kinds of harpoons, but the one that was most effective by far was the one invented by African American blacksmith Lewis Temple. His "toggle harpoon" was mounted on a pivot, which greatly decreased the chance that it would work its way loose once it was embedded in the whale. The number of harpoons used in the whaling industry was immense, best exemplified by the fact that one blacksmith alone, James Durfee of New Bedford, made and sold 58,517 harpoons.

No matter what types of whales they were after, whalemen were in constant peril when attacking the creatures, especially at the moment they drew close enough for the whale to be killed with a lance.

he was now into dying convulsions and ran around in a circle; but his flurry was soon over; he turned upon his left side, and floated dead. We gave three hearty cheers, and took him in tow for the ship, which was now fifteen miles off."

Fifteen miles off! For the green hands, having survived their first encounter with a whale, the ordeal of securing a hook to either the jaw or the flukes of a more than fifty-ton animal and then towing it behind a light whaleboat for such an incredible distance was yet another introduction to the hardships of whaling. From the moment they towed their first whale back to the whaleship, all would heartily agree with the whaleman who long ago had stated, "Of all the ungainly things to tow, a dead sperm whale is the worst. You can stick your oar two or three times into the same hole in the ocean before making any progress."

As difficult, tiring, and dangerous as capturing a sperm whale was, it was only the first of two steps in the whaling process. The second involved extracting the oil from the whale, a procedure that, in many ways, was as dangerous as chasing and killing the beasts.

As soon as the whale was towed back to the ship, it was secured to the side of the vessel with heavy chains.

All aboard knew that it was important to process the animal as quickly as possible. One never knew when a violent storm might tear the creature away from the ship. Sharks were also a constant nuisance. The blood from the whale's wounds attracted them in droves, and every gigantic bite they took meant less oil for the whalemen.

Once the whale was in place, crewmen erected a large platform, called a cutting stage, directly above the whale. Then the captain and first mate went out onto the stage, no small feat on the side of a wave-tossed vessel, and with sharp cutting spades separated the whale's head from its body. By using block and tackle, other crew members hauled the enormous head onto the deck. "It was [amazing] to me to see how well they could part the head from the body and find the joint so nicely," Eliza Williams wrote in one of her journals. "When it came on deck, it was such a large head, it swung against the side of the ship till [the vessel] seemed to shake with the weight of it."

The sperm whale's head was particularly valuable because inside it lay a huge reservoir of oil. But this was not all. Inside it also was a huge amount of a pulpy substance called spermaceti, out of which, in a time before electricity, the world's finest candles were made.

The head of a sperm might be so large that in order to get at the oil and spermaceti most efficiently, crewmen, once the head was cut open, actually went down inside it to carry out the task. It was called "bailing out the case," and it was a sight that few who saw it for the first time would ever forget. "Stark naked, three [crewmen] climbed into its tank-like interior, and wallowing to their waists, with knives and scoops, half cut, half ladled the barrels of pulpy, dripping substance from its cells," wrote whaleman Clifford Ashley. "Delving deeper and deeper with an eagerness requiring no encouragement, the bailers labored without cessation." Whaleman Robert Weir described it this way: "Wouldn't this be a rich scene for the dear ones at home to see. A couple of men buried in a whale head — a delightful situation surely."

It might have been a "delightful situation" to Weir, but most of the crew had no time to watch the bailing take place. They were too busy beginning the main task of the processing operation, that of stripping the tons of blubber from the whale so that the oil within it could be extracted.

LEFT: It took strength and considerable dexterity to cut the enormously heavy strips of blubber from the whale while standing on the narrow, slippery cutting stage that extended out from the ever-rocking whaleship.

"There is a murderous appearance about the blood-stained decks, and the huge masses of flesh and blubber lying here and there," John Ross Browne recalled. "And, along with the flesh and blubber, there was the oil that had not gone into the barrels." "The whole ship is bathed in oil," whaling chronicler Frances Robotti wrote. "The decks are sliding with it. The men are covered with it. The oil is in their hair, on their eyelids, in their ears, under their fingernails, soaked through their shoes and every thread of their clothes. Their food is permeated with it. Their sleeping bunks are drenched with it. Perhaps the only way they endure the drudgery of grease and grime is the recollection of the high excitement of the chase and capture."

Even with oil stored safely in the hold, the work was not done. Now the ship had to be scrubbed and made as clean as possible. It was a seemingly endless routine from the first "Thar she blows" to the tedious wash-down of the vessel.

For the men and women of the 1871 fleet, it was all a prelude to what was to come. For four months they had chased the sperm whales and had filled their barrels with thousands of gallons of oil. The green hands were "greenies" no longer. Most had become excellent oarsmen. All had experienced the thrills and terrors of hunting creatures larger and more frightening than they could have imagined. What they didn't know was that these frightening experiences would pale in comparison to what lay ahead.

Life on a Whaleship

---- ◎ ----

THE AVERAGE CREW of a whaleship consisted of thirty-five or thirty-six men organized into a rigid class structure. At the top was the captain, who was the absolute master of the ship. Next came the three or four mates, each of whom commanded a whaleboat. Following them in rank came the harpooners, who were given more privileges than the other crewmen. The blacksmith, cook, carpenter, cooper, and steward also ranked higher than the ordinary seamen who made up the rest of the crew.

This class structure was particularly reflected in where the men lived and ate. The captain had his own cabin at the rear of the ship, complete with sofa and chairs. He was served much better food than anyone else on board. The mates had smaller cabins in the rear of the vessel and ate their meals with the captain in his quarters. The harpooners, blacksmith, cook, carpenter, and cooper had bunks in a compartment in the middle of the ship and ate their meals in the captain's cabin after the mates had left.

The rest of the crew — the ordinary seamen — slept in bunks and ate their meals in a narrow, triangular-shaped room under the deck in the front of the ship. Their sea chests were their only seats. While the captain and mates often dined on duck, pork, or chicken, the ordinary seamen were served much less luxurious fare.

They had to satisfy the hearty appetites their work gave them with heavily salted beef, hard biscuits, beans, rice, and potatoes, all washed down with tea or coffee so weak that it was difficult to tell the difference between them. The only breaks in the monotonous diet came when a whaleship was fortunate enough to put into a port during a voyage. Until they ran out, such treats as fresh fruits and vegetables, and even fresh water, boosted the spirits of all the men.

CHAPTER FOUR

Disaster Strikes

. . . THICK WEATHER, the ship lying fast to the grounded ice. Thirty ships in sight at anchor and fast to the grounded ice and closed in between the land and the ice with no possibility of getting out for the present . . . — a poor prospect.

— *Log of the* Seneca, *September 3, 1871*

By the middle of May, most of the ships had arrived in Arctic waters. Behind them were the warmer seas and the temperate winds. The sperm whales too had been left behind. Now it was time to hunt the bowheads, to fill the vessels with the whalebone the ships had come so far to obtain.

The green hands on every vessel became aware of the differences as soon as the first bowheads were spotted. The shouts that came from the lookouts were no longer "Thar she blows" or "She blows," but "There go flu-u-u-ukes, flukes," tribute to the bowheads' most visible and dangerous weapon.

The processing of the whale also took on a new dimension. Although less so than in previous times, whale oil was still profitable, and once a bowhead was killed and towed back to the ship, the stripping of the whale's blubber (called "cutting-in") and the same boiling down of the blubber into oil (called "trying-out") took place. But to the captains and crews of the fleet, it was the baleen in the bowhead's enormous mouth that was most valuable. In his journal, Arctic whaling captain Harty Bodfish described how these enormous slabs of bone were extracted once the whale's head was chopped from its body and hauled on deck. "The men go around [the head] cleaning away the blubber and cutting the muscle that holds the bone. Continuous strain as the tackles lifts the head and when the [baleen] is clear, it will fall to the deck spread out flat. . . . After this is done, the skull is hove overboard and the men knock the 'oysters' or muscles and gum fragments from the slabs of bone with heads of axes. Then it is bundled up, four or five slabs in a bundle, and stowed below or on deck, wherever it is convenient. Later it must be washed or scraped to remove all the gum."

To the green hands in particular, one of the greatest changes from the initiation they received into whaling in the lower latitudes was the change in the number of hours they were now required to be at work. Most, having arrived in the Arctic in the spring, were astounded to find that it remained light twenty-four hours a day. Whaling was to be carried out continuously. So too was the cutting-in, trying-out, and the extraction and processing of the bone.

But whether it was during normal daytime or the Arctic's light-filled nighttime hours, all of those who manned the whaleboats once a bowhead was sighted became quickly aware of the special dangers involved in pursuing the creatures. Among the first members of the fleet to witness what could happen was William Fish Williams, Captain Thomas Williams's cabin-boy son. He would later write:

I have already remarked that the bowhead is not [as great a fighter as the sperm whale], but I do not want you to infer from this statement that there is no risk involved in their capture. For like everything else connected with the sea, you pass so quickly from comedy to tragedy, and from tragedy to comedy, that you are never safe in trying to limit the possible dangers in the capture of a whale. . . .

One of the whales taken by our boats . . . proceeded literally to spank it, bringing its great flukes down on top of the boat several times. From [where I stood on] the ship it looked very bad for the crew and the boat, but aside from a broken oar or two no real damage was done to either and the whale was killed. Of course the crew hugged the bottom of the boat pretty close, but the real secret of the escape was the fact that the whale [did not attack again]. . . .

Another time my father's boat was fast to a whale that was running for the . . . ice, when by a sudden swerve in his course he ran the boat over a small cake of ice, capsizing the boat and running off with the line. Before we on shipboard could hardly realize what had happened [my father and] the boat's crew were all sitting astride the keel [which was all that remained of the boat]. Fortunately the line did not catch on anything, and what might have been a tragedy became a farce, and one that for some time it was not good judgment to discuss within the hearing of my father.

The ice that Williams mentioned in his account would not have been a surprising part of his story had the incident in which his father was involved taken place later in the year. But these events occurred in early June, only three weeks after the ships had reached the Arctic. Even those members of the fleet who had sailed to the region before were surprised to encounter ice so early in the whaling season. An even greater surprise lay immediately ahead.

On a day when several of the ships were either cutting-in or trying-out, some five or six miles from shore, crew members suddenly spotted Eskimos paddling out to their vessels in sealskin-covered boats called umiaks.

In the spring, these first North American whalemen used their umiaks to pursue whales relatively close to shore. They were the first in the New World to use harpoons to latch onto the whales, and the first to use lances to kill them once they were harpooned. After a whale was killed, it was hauled up onto the ice. Then the entire Eskimo community went out onto the frozen surface, where each member cut off as much of the whale as he or she could haul ashore by sled. Everything that could be used for food, building materials, fuel, or summer trade with people farther inland (who coveted whale oil) was stripped away.

The fact that Eskimos had come out to the ships was not, in itself, alarming. It was not unusual for vessels that were whaling within a few miles of the shore to receive such a visit. But this time, instead of their usual greetings, the natives arrived with dire warnings. The weather ahead, they told the whalemen, would be far more severe than normal. To make matters worse, they added, the winter season, bringing with it severe storms and the relentless buildup of ice, would descend upon the Arctic much earlier than in previous years.

Most of the whaling fleet's captains listened politely to what the Eskimos had to say but were not overly concerned. The majority of them regarded the natives as childlike people whose lives were ruled not by reality, but by superstition. What were they supposed to do — abandon these rich whaling grounds that they had traveled so far to reach? How would they ever be able to explain to the owners of their vessels that they had done so on the advice of these primitive people? They felt the Eskimos could be simply wrong: Perhaps this winter would be unusually severe, but the waters couldn't possibly freeze over before September. By that time the captains would have filled their ships with bone and sailed home to a triumphant return.

Some of the captains, however, were not so sure. They knew that these natives and their ancestors had lived for thousands of years in this region and understood every weather sign. It was a time of decisions, and after many deliberations seven of the fleet's captains decided that it would be wise to heed the Eskimos' predictions. Soon after the natives left their ships, they set out to whale some eighty miles southward, where they were sure the waters were less likely to freeze over prematurely.

Putting the warnings out of their minds, the crews of the remaining thirty-two ships continued whaling in waters off the region's Point Belcher (close to the northernmost part of modern Alaska). Although the whaling was good, they were surprised when within a month the temperature dropped sharply and even heavier ice packs began to form. But they were much too busy to be concerned with the weather.

Not so, however, the men of the *Oriole*. As they went about their business on a particularly foggy June day, they were, without warning, thrown to the deck to the accompaniment of a sickening, wrenching sound as their ship was struck by a giant ice pack. As they looked on in horror, the sides of the vessel began to cave in, forcing them to sail into a nearby bay. There they discovered that the ship was too badly damaged to be repaired. Leaving the vessel behind, the crew of the *Oriole* was distributed among the other ships. The whaling fleet of 1871 had suffered its first casualty.

Almost immediately afterward, some of the other ships began to feel the effects of the surprisingly early buildup of ice and the relentless southwest winds that kept moving the ice toward where the ships were whaling. One of these vessels was the *Monticello*, aboard which William Fish Williams had already been introduced to the challenges of the Arctic. "It was blowing quite fresh," he would later recall, "and the ice had suddenly shifted.

We were practically cut off from open water except for a narrow passage between two very large floes of ice . . . we had no alternative except to try to make it [through the passage]. The ship first struck [the ice] a glancing blow on the bow . . . then shearing off she ran directly into the floe on the other side, which she struck with tremendous force, bringing her to a complete stop and throwing the [men] below out of their berths. After a few heavy rolls she gathered headway and went through the passage. Of course we thought she was [caved in]. The pumps were immediately rigged and men sent down below . . . to see if they could hear the water coming in, but soon they reported everything quiet and pumps confirmed the report but it was a narrow escape."

The *Monticello* was not alone in its difficulties. In mid-July, Captain Leander Owen's *Contest* had a hole torn in its bow when it was struck by ice. Fortunately the damage was just high enough above the waterline to permit repairs to be made. A month later, when chasing whales in a heavy fog, the same vessel lost its bearings and ran aground. Only the strenuous efforts of the crews of the *Oliver Crocker* and the *Massachusetts*, who assisted in refloating the vessel, kept the *Contest* from being permanently beached.

And the problems continued. Less than a week after the *Contest's* latest near calamity, several of the ships spotted whales and lowered their whaleboats to give chase. To their disappointment, the men in the boats were unable to capture any of the creatures, which was only the beginning of their difficulties. When they were returning to the ships, they suddenly became caught in thick ice.

It was incredible. The fleet was encountering what their captains had never thought possible. They were being seriously threatened by midwinter Arctic conditions, and winter was still a long way off. Increasingly the captains' logs began to reflect the situation. "Found ourselves among thick, heavy ice," wrote Horace Newbury, "and the fog so thick that at times we could hardly see a ship's length off."

Amazingly, through it all, they were still catching whales. But they were doing so in a way that none of the captains and crewmen had ever done before. There was now so much heavy ice in the water that when whales were spotted, the ships could not safely sail toward the creatures before lowering their whaleboats. Instead, the crews had to haul the boats over the ice packs to open water before setting out in pursuit. To make matters more difficult, the clever bowheads instinctively felt safe in the ice. Soon the whalemen were seeing and hearing far more whales than they were able to catch. "Struck a whale five miles from the ship," the *Henry Taber*'s mate wrote in his log. "Whale ran under the ice. Lost line. . . . Saw him no more."

Because the large ice packs made it impossible to tow the huge creatures back to the ship, the crew had to spend long hours on the freezing ice cutting a whale apart before towing the blubber miles back to the ship.

To make matters even worse, the unprecedented procedure was so time-consuming that in order to complete their tasks, the crews often had to sleep either on the ice or on the shore until the job was done. For the first time many crewmen, particularly those engaged in their first whaling venture, began to seriously question the wisdom of having signed aboard.

On August 29 the wind shifted to the southwest, bringing with it the fiercest storm the fleet had yet encountered. Driven by the relentless wind, an almost

---

By the end of August 1871, the Eskimos' warning that by continuing to whale off Point Belcher the fleet risked becoming trapped in ice had become all too true.

The Whaleship

———— ◉ ————

IN AN AGE when tens of thousands of tall-masted ships plied the oceans of the world, whaleships were particularly distinctive vessels. At sea, a whaleship was distinguished by its slow speed, its lookouts standing high in its masts, the whaleboats hanging from its sides, and the smoke often billowing from the brick furnace called a tryworks where the whales' blubber was boiled down. If it was in the middle of a successful voyage, it could also often be identified by the smell of oil that emanated from it, leading other types of seamen to state, "You can smell a whaleship long before you see it."

The average whaleship was about one hundred feet long and had a carrying capacity of more than three hundred tons. It was not built to look sleek or to outrace other ships. Rather, it was designed to provide ample deck space for processing the captured whales and to be large enough to store as many barrels of oil and bundles of whalebone as possible in its hold. Because it spent a longer time at sea than any other vessel, and because it had to be strong enough to handle the tons of blubber hoisted onto its deck, a whaleship had to be as sturdy as its builders could make it.

They may have smelled bad, and they may not have been as graceful-looking as most other types of sailing ships. But the whaleships did their job, and before their days were over, they wrote a bold and unique chapter in the nation's history.

endless chain of enormous ice packs moved steadily closer to the ships, forcing them to retreat nearer and nearer to the land. Soon the vessels were scattered all up and down the coast with nothing but an unbroken mass of ice between them and water along the shore. More than 1,200 people were now trapped in ice.

The consequences were almost immediate. On September 1 ice packs that had broken away from the main mass slammed into the *Eugenia*, snapping off her anchor and chain, driving the vessel toward the beach. Working feverishly, the ship's crew was able to haul up another anchor and chain from the hold. They were only three-quarters of a mile from being driven up onto the land when they managed to drop the new anchor and save the vessel from being beached.

"Some twenty-six sail in sight," the *Eugenia*'s mate confided to his log. "All jammed in the ice close to the beach. Things look bad at present." The *Eugenia* was not alone in its plight. The day after that ship's crew had performed its heroics, the lookout of the *Henry Taber* spotted an alarming sight. The *Comet* was flying its ship's flag at half-mast, a signal that the vessel was in serious trouble. Immediately the *Henry Taber*'s captain ordered a boat lowered, and he and members of his crew headed for the *Comet*. As soon as they reached the vessel, they were sickened by what they saw. Every one of the whaleship's huge timbers — which, on many voyages, had weathered the heaviest seas — was completely shattered. Most of the *Comet*'s crew had sought refuge in the vessel's whaleboats. Others were standing on the ice. More boats were then dispatched from the *Henry Taber*, and the *Comet*'s crew was rescued and divided among the other ships of the fleet. For three full days the wreck of the *Comet* was suspended end on end between two gigantic masses of ice, its stern pointing skyward, reminding all who could see it of how serious the situation had become. Finally, tide and current moved the ice that had crushed the ship, and the *Comet* slipped beneath the sea.

Yet even with this disaster, there were still many aboard the ships who held out hope that things would once again improve. Aboard many of the vessels, in fact, there were those hardy whalemen who, having survived other horrific experiences at sea, were more concerned over when they could resume whaling than they were over the dangerous ice.

But they were wrong. Day by day the ice kept building up, further imprisoning the fleet. Then on September 3, the *Roman* suffered the same fate as the *Comet*. Squeezed from all sides by heavy ice, the ship suddenly splintered apart. Within forty-five minutes, as its captain, mates, and crew fled across the ice for their lives, what was left of the *Roman* sank to the bottom. As if this was not catastrophe enough, five days later the *Ashawonks* was destroyed by ice. Lying in shallow water, it did not sink, but its wreckage remained as a vivid reminder of what had befallen the once-confident fleet.

Shaken by these latest calamities, even the most optimistic of the whalemen realized that they were now in real peril. "Nearly everyone in the fleet despairs of getting their ships [out] which is a cause of much uneasiness," the *Henry Taber*'s mate wrote. Horace Newbury's log contained even more ominous words. "Unless a change of wind takes place soon," it read, "all are lost."

Newbury's fellow captains shared his feelings. They were now all too aware that the issue was no longer that of whether they would be able to continue whaling but that of whether or not 1,219 people would survive. They knew also that the magnitude of the situation was one that no other whaling captain had ever faced. "We felt keenly our responsibility, with three million dollars worth of property and [more than] 1,200 lives at stake," wrote the *Gay Head*'s Captain William Kelley. "Young ice forms nearly every night and the land was covered with snow. There was every indication that winter had set in."

Faced with this responsibility, the captains of the whaleships gathered together on the *Champion* for the first of what would be a series of agonizing meetings. They agreed that the chances of the ships getting out to clear water before spring was very remote — and spring was at least seven months away. They were aware that the provisions they had stored aboard for the short Arctic whaling season would last no more than three months. And they knew that surviving the winter on the shore would be nothing short of impossible.

But they refused to panic. They would try everything possible, hoping somehow they would find a way out. To a man they agreed that their best chance of making it was by establishing contact with the seven ships that had heeded the Eskimos' warnings and had gone whaling farther south, and pleading with them for rescue.

The captains had seen that there was a narrow channel of water between their ships and the solid ice packs. It seemed to stretch out toward the open waters off Icy Cape, where they believed the seven ships that had gone south were whaling. They decided to begin their quest for survival by seeing if this passageway was deep enough for two of the lightest ships in the fleet, the *Kohola* and the *Victoria*, to travel through. If they were, and if the channel stretched outward and was passable all the way to Icy Cape, they would perhaps be able, by making repeated trips in the two vessels, to get everyone to Icy Cape in the hope that the seven ships were still there and would rescue them.

But these were two very big *ifs*. The captains had no way of knowing if the passageway extended the long eighty miles to Icy Cape. Even if it did, would they be able to lighten the *Kohola* and the *Victoria* sufficiently so that the two ships would rise high enough out of the water to be floated over the icy sandbar next to which they were trapped and then guided into the channel?

The captains knew that they had to find the answers to these questions as quickly as possible. Led by Thomas Williams and William Kelley, scores of crewmen labored for hours hoisting every cask of oil, every provision, and everything else that could be removed out of the two ships in order to make them as light as possible. But it was all in vain. Despite their efforts, the now almost-empty ships still did not rise high enough to be floated over the bar.

With the weather getting worse every day and with time rapidly running out, the captains immediately went to work on a second plan. They decided to send three whaleboats, led by the *Florida*'s Captain D. R. Fraser, down the channel to see if they could accomplish what could not be done with the *Kohola* and the *Victoria*.

With snow pounding down upon them and with chunks of ice floating in the passageway, Fraser and his party climbed into the boats and departed. As the three open vessels moved out of sight, the hopes and prayers of everyone in the fleet went with them. All knew that Fraser and his men probably represented their last chance of staying alive. They asked themselves the same questions. Would Fraser make it all the way to Icy Cape? Were the seven ships still there? And if they were, would they be willing to abandon their whaling and pack 1,219 people aboard their vessels? The very real possibility that Fraser might never return or would find that the seven whaleships had left the region was almost too horrible to contemplate. What would they do then?

Some of the captains felt that their only remaining option would be to try to take everyone in the whaleboats down the passageway to open seas, and then across the Arctic Ocean to the nearest port. Other captains felt that this would be nothing short of suicide. "For my part," stated Captain Dexter of the *Emily Morgan*, "I will not cross the Arctic Ocean in an open whaleboat laden with men and provisions in the latter part of September and October. . . . Out of [more than] twelve hundred, not a hundred will survive." Dexter and some of his colleagues were convinced that should Fraser prove unsuccessful, the 1,219 members of the fleet would have to try taking their chances by living out the winter on the shore near where their ships were trapped. They were certain that the majority would die, but perhaps some would be able to survive. One thing was certain: Their only real hope lay with Fraser.

RIGHT: The lookouts perched high above the deck usually scanned the seas for whales, but after Captain Fraser went off in search of rescue vessels, their job became that of awaiting the hoped-for sight of his return.

CHAPTER FIVE

Fleeing for Their Lives

RESCUE, EVEN IF there were somebody to the south willing to try it, was no sure thing. Everybody [in the fleet] knew it.

— *Everett S. Allen,* Children of the Light, *1973*

By September 12, Fraser and his men had been gone for four days. Aboard the icebound ships hope was rapidly fading as everyone nervously wondered what had happened to them. Had they found that the channel was not open all the way to Icy Cape? Had they made it all the way, only to find that they could not get back to the fleet because of new ice that had formed in the channel? Or had they suffered an even more calamitous fate?

But suddenly there were cries from the lookouts atop one of the ships. Three battered whaleboats, with Fraser at the bow of the lead vessel, were making their way up the channel toward the fleet. Immediately the anxious captains called a meeting on the *Champion* to hear what Fraser had discovered.

As soon as the drenched and exhausted Fraser climbed aboard the *Champion*, he gave his report. The passageway, he told the captains, was open all the way to Icy Cape. But new ice, he also told them, was already forming all along the channel. The three whaleboats had, in fact, been continuously struck by floating ice and had been badly damaged. Furthermore, Fraser stated, there was the very real possibility that much of the narrow passageway would freeze over before another week was out, shutting off the only route of escape.

But Fraser had other news as well — news that everyone in the whaling fleet had been waiting to hear. Fraser and his expedition had not only made it all the way to the waters off Icy Cape, but the seven whaleships were still there. Best news of all: Fraser had made contact with one of the vessels, the *Progress*, whose captain, James Dowden, had listened incredulously as he was told of the whaling fleet's desperate situation. Then Fraser repeated what Dowden had said to him upon hearing the news. "Tell them all," Dowden had exclaimed, "I will wait for them as long as I have an anchor left or a spar to carry a sail."

Upon hearing Fraser's report and Captain Dowden's response to their plight, even the most hardened of the fleet's captains could not help but be overcome with emotion. It was certainly the best news they could have expected to hear. But it was tempered by what they knew lay ahead. They would have to abandon the ships, would have to pack all 1,219 men, women, and children into the more than two hundred whaleboats that still remained, and would have to try to make it all the way down the channel, not knowing whether or not it was still open. And they would have to do it while hoping that the seven whaleships would still be waiting there and would attempt to rescue them once they arrived.

Each of the captains was all too aware that the plan was fraught with both known and unknown dangers and possible catastrophe. Would more than 1,200 people, including women and young children, be able to survive an eighty-mile journey in open boats in below-zero temperatures while being assailed by snow and hail and storm-force winds? Would some of the boats be crushed by ice floes, tossing their occupants into the freezing water, where they would surely die? Would they get partway down the passageway only to find that the waters ahead, as Fraser had predicted, had become completely frozen over? And there was another painful consideration. The captains knew that the ocean off Icy Cape was particularly storm-tossed, characterized by unusually high waves. Even if what seemed impossible happened and all of the boats made it all the way to the open sea, would the seven ships be able to accomplish a successful rescue in the treacherous ocean waters?

It was a horrendous decision to have to make, but the captains were convinced that it was their best and, in fact, their only option. One can only imagine what thoughts and emotions ran through them all as they voted unanimously to abandon the ships. These were men who, for most of their lives, had dedicated themselves to rewarding the owners of their ships with profitable voyages. To them the greatest of all disgraces was to return to port with their ships not filled to capacity with oil and whalebone. Now they would be returning not only without oil and bone, but without the ships themselves — if they were lucky enough to return at all.

The captains had seen four of their vessels totally destroyed. They had only to look around them to view the twenty-eight other ships helplessly locked in the ice. Day by day they had seen the concerned expressions on the faces of all those aboard the ships. But what about those back home, let alone people around the world? Would those who were not eyewitness to the disaster ever be able to comprehend the severity of the situation? Instead would they feel that the captains had disgraced themselves by panicking and running away from their ships?

For these proud and dedicated men, it was perhaps the most anguishing consideration of all. With these thoughts in mind, the captains decided to write a letter to the world, explaining the reasons for their decision, a letter they hoped they would live to deliver back home. It read:

Know ye all men that we the undersigned, masters of whaleships, ... after holding a meeting cerning our dreadful situation, have all come to the conclusion that our ships cannot be got out this year and there being no harbor that we can get our vessels into and not having provisions enough to feed our crews to exceed three months and being in a barren country where there is neither food nor fuel to be obtained, we feel ourselves under the painful necessity of abandoning our vessels and trying to work our way south with our boats and if possible get on board ships that are south of the ice.

We think it would not be prudent to leave a single soul to look after our vessels as the first westerly gale will crowd the ice ashore and either crush the ships or drive them high upon the beach. Three of the fleet have already been crushed and two are now lying hove out, which have been crushed by the ice and are leaking badly. . . . Should we be cast on the beach, it would be at least eleven months before we could look for assistance, and in all probability, nine out of ten would die of starvation . . . before the opening of spring.

Therefore, we have arrived at these conclusions after the return of our expedition under the command of Captain D. R. Fraser of the Florida, *he, having with whaleboats worked to the southward [to Icy Cape], and found that the ice pressed ashore the entire distance from our position to [Icy Cape], leaving in several places only sufficient water for our boats to pass through and this liable at any moment to be frozen over during the [next] twenty-four hours, which would cut off our retreat, even by the boats, as Captain Fraser had to work through a considerable quantity of young ice during his expedition, which cut up his boats badly.*

Even after writing this detailed letter, the masters felt that there was yet another document that needed to be composed. They had been gratified, to say the least, by Captain Dowden's assurance that his ship, *Progress*, and the other six whaleships to the south would wait to take the members of the fleet aboard their vessels. As whaling captains themselves, they were aware of the enormity of the sacrifice they were asking the masters of the seven vessels to the south to make. During their days at sea, they had all come into contact with whaling captains who might simply have turned their backs on the imperiled fleet rather than give up the prospect of a profitable voyage. Knowing that it would be beneficial to the masters of the seven vessels to have written proof of the necessity of turning aside profits in order to rescue them, the captains had Captain Henry Pease create a document acknowledging the sacrifice they knew they were asking their fellow captains to make. It read:

Gentlemen:

. . . By a meeting of all the masters of the vessels which are [trapped] by the ice along this shore . . . I am requested to make known to you our deplorable situation and ask your assistance. We have for the last fifteen days been satisfied that there is not the slightest possibility of saving any of our ships or their property, in view of the fact that the northern barrier of ice has set permanently on this shore, shutting in all the fleet north of Icy Cape, leaving only a narrow belt of water from one-quarter to one-half mile in width

extending from Point Belcher to south of Icy Cape. . . . The water [is] in no place of sufficient depth to float our lightest . . . vessels. . . .

Counting the crews of the four wrecked ships, we number some twelve hundred souls, with not more than three months' provisions and fuel; no clothing suitable for winter wear. All attempts to pass the winter here would be suicidal. Not more than two hundred out of the twelve would survive to tell the sufferings of the others.

Looking our deplorable situation squarely in the face, we feel convinced that to save the lives of our crews, a speedy abandonment of our ships is necessary. A change of wind to the north for twenty-four hours would cause the young ice to make so stout as to effectively close up the narrow passage and cut off our retreat by boats.

We realize your peculiar situation as to duty, and the bright prospects you have for a good catch in oil and bone before the season expires; and now call on you, in the voice of

humanity to abandon your whaling, sacrifice
your personal interest as well as that of your
owners, and put yourselves in condition to
receive on board ourselves and crews for transit
to some civilized port. . . .

We are respectfully yours, Henry Pease Jr.,
with thirty-one other masters.

Having completed their difficult writing tasks, the captains, knowing that they had not a moment to spare, ordered that all of their ships be abandoned the following day. Alone in his cabin, Captain Leander Owen wrote some of the saddest words he had ever entered into one of his many logs. "September 13," it read. "Several meetings were held today to discuss affairs and it was decided to fix tomorrow at 10 A.M., to abandon the ships." Owen was a man of few words and his was a typically simple statement to describe a decision that would send 1,219 people off on what they all knew would be a terrifying journey whose outcome was very much in doubt.

To no one's surprise, there was very little sleep aboard any of the ships the night of the thirteenth, and early the next day everyone, including the women and most of the children, were at work preparing to leave the ships and enter the whaleboats. "Finished fitting our boats and making preparations to flee for our lives," the *Henry Taber*'s first mate wrote in his log. Captain Horace Newbury's entry was as brief and to the point as Leander Owen's had been. "At 10 A.M. let go of the second anchor and veered out 50 fathoms on port chain and 30 on starboard. At 2 P.M. abandoned the ship."

Some of the last log entries that would ever be written aboard the ships, however, were more emotional. "With sad hearts ordered all the men into the boats and with a last look over the decks, abandoned the ship to the mercy of the elements," wrote the *Emily Morgan*'s first mate, William Earle. "All hope of saving the ship or property is gone. If we save our lives, we ought to be satisfied and that should satisfy the world."

Aside from the emotional strain, abandoning the ships was far from an easy task. Because the vessels were completely surrounded by ice, the whaleboats had to be dragged over the uneven frozen surface and then carefully placed in the narrow passage that all hoped would be their avenue to salvation.

Once in the boats, the thoughts of what they were leaving behind came full force upon almost everyone aboard. "I doubt if I can adequately describe the leave-taking of our ship," William Fish Williams would later write. "It was depressing enough to me ... but to my father and mother it must have been a [particularly] sad parting, and I think what made it still more so was the fact that only a short distance from our [vessel, the *Monticello*,] lay the ship *Florida* of which my father had [previously] commanded for eight years and on which three of his children had been born. The usual abandonment of a ship is the result of some irreparable injury and is executed in great haste; but here we were leaving a ship that was absolutely sound, that had been our home for nearly ten months and had taken us safely through many a trying time."

Shortly after the captains had made the decision to abandon the ships, they had ordered the crew of every vessel to add long strips of sturdy wood to the sides of each of the whaleboats that would be taken down the channel. Hopefully, the heightening of the sides would help keep everyone from being tossed out if their boats were struck violently by ice. Crew members had also covered the bow of each boat with copper sheathing, another precaution against floating ice.

While this was being done, the captains had given

another command, one in keeping with seafaring tradition. They had ordered that the ships' flags be hoisted and flown upside down, an ages-old signal of abandonment. Now, as each of the whaleboats passed by the vessels, each person aboard gazed mournfully at the flags. Even more wrenching was the sight of the ships themselves. To these men of the sea, there was nothing more inspiring than a tall-masted ship, its huge sails billowing in the wind, cutting its way through the ocean. But the last sight they would ever have of their fleet was a lasting image of motionless vessels, their sails lowered, their decks and whaleboat mounts empty, standing not in water but in a solid mass of snow-covered ice.

It was, to say the least, a mournful sight. However, there was little time to reflect upon it. There were almost two hundred whaleboats, some with their sails up, now beginning to make their way down the channel, and everyone's attention had to be focused on what lay ahead. "One of the boats being very slow," wrote William Earle, "our progress was not very rapid. . . . Hundreds of boats were ahead of us, as far as the eye could see."

Being delayed by slow-moving boats was a real problem. They all knew that they were battling time as well as the elements. Captain Fraser's warning that the passageway closer to Icy Cape might freeze completely over was never out of their thoughts. And every moment lost meant another moment when the seven vessels that they hoped would receive them might be forced by ice storms to move away.

Because time was such a factor, it had been decided before they left that they would travel by night as well as by day. The captains hoped that by doing so, all of the boats, barring catastrophe, would reach Icy Cape in two days. It was yet another risky decision. Spotting obstacles in the passageway in the daylight was difficult enough; avoiding them in the blackness of night was an even greater challenge.

Remarkably, along with carrying out his responsibilities as leader of his whaleboat, William Earle also somehow managed to jot down hastily scribbled notes describing what his journey down the passageway was like, particularly after it became dark. "As night came on," Earle wrote, "the wind increased and as darkness closed around us, heavy black clouds seemed to rest over us and it was not possible to see more than a few feet and we were in constant danger of coming in collision with the many fragments of ice floating in the narrow passage."

The Whaleboat

———— ◉ ————

OF ALL THE VARIOUS TYPES of equipment, large and small, that enabled the whalemen to ply their trade, the most important of all was the whaleboat. Termed "a poem of its kind" by whaling historian Everett S. Allen and lauded by generations of nautical experts as the most perfectly designed of all vessels, the whaleboat was eloquently described by Captain William Davis, a man who had traveled hundreds of miles in the light, speedy, and graceful craft.

"The whaleboat," Davis wrote, "is simply as perfect as the combined skill of the millions of men who have risked life and limb in [whaling] service could make it. [It] is 28 feet long, sharp and clean cut as a dolphin, . . . with a bottom round and buoyant . . . [its] rise of bow and stern, with [its] clipper-like upper form, gives it a duck-like capacity to top the oncoming waves so that it will dryly ride when ordinary boats would fill. . . . Here we have a craft that can make ten miles an hour in dead chase by the oars alone."

The many necessary articles carried in each whaleboat, aside from the six whalers who manned it, included: two wooden tubs, each containing 900 feet of carefully coiled line; two harpoons ready for use, and two or three spares; a hatchet and knives to cut the lines in an emergency; two or three lances; a compass; a long-poled flag called a waif, used to mark where a whale, once killed, was floating; and a small bucket called a piggin, used to pour water on the line should it begin to smoke or even catch fire when dragged for miles by a harpooned whale.

By around 10:00 P.M. most of the boats had been in the channel almost twelve hours. All aboard were exhausted. Concerned particularly about the women and children, who had been hanging on for dear life to the sides of the boats for hours, the captains in the lead whaleboats decided that all should put ashore for at least a short period of rest.

By now the weather was even worse than it had been when they abandoned the ships. As the hundreds of drenched, weary souls stumbled ashore, men from the boats that had already landed scoured the sparse beach area for whatever driftwood they could find so that fires could be made. Other whalemen dragged some of the boats ashore and, by covering them with sails, made shelters for the women and children. The rest of the fleet members tried to get what little rest they could.

It was a temporary respite at best. The weather continued to deteriorate and, as the temperatures continued to drop, the captains and mates knew that every hour spent on the beach was an hour in which ice would be building up in the channel. Soon, many of the boats were back in the water. "At 10:30 P.M., landed by a fire on the shore where several boats were hauled up and made some coffee," wrote William Earle.

While we were on shore, the wind began to increase ... shoved off into the darkness at 11:30. The navigation was difficult and dangerous. We kept [trying to avoid bumping into ice on one side of us and land on the other and continuously checked the depth of the water].

The [wind] lasted until about 1:30 A.M. with a darkness almost black. Just as the wind began to die away, one of our boats came in contact with a small piece of ice, staving a hole in her bow. She hauled up on the beach and the hole being fortunately above water was soon repaired.... Sent up rockets and ... proceeded ... on our way. At 7 A.M. hauled up to [another] beach, landed and made coffee and took breakfast with what appetite may be imagined. At 8 embarked again."

Earle's difficulties were typical of the troubles that many of the occupants of the boats were having. Their faces were continually being struck by wind-driven sleet. Many were finding that their hands and feet were becoming numb from the cold. Some were experiencing the first stages of frostbite. Even for those like Henry Pease, Leander Owen, Thomas and Eliza Williams and their children, and other members of the desperate expedition who had suffered previous Arctic disasters, the trip was becoming increasingly difficult to bear. Yet, having no other choice, they moved relentlessly on, and by the middle of the second day almost all the boats were only some twenty miles from Icy Cape. But now the captains had another serious worry. They had been traveling practically nonstop for more than thirty-six hours. Many of the men at the oars had been rowing almost the entire time. Even if the passageway remained open, would all those aboard the boats have enough energy left to battle the much stormier seas around Icy Cape? It was a real concern, one that would have been even greater had they known that, all the while, the seven ships that they hoped to find waiting for them had been having potentially disastrous problems of their own.

On September 1, a full two weeks before the decision to abandon the stricken fleet had been made, the seven vessels to the south had suddenly found themselves blocked by so much ice that they had to anchor near the shore in water so shallow they could barely float.

For the next two days they too had been trapped in ice. Fortunately on the eleventh the ice began to shift, allowing the seven vessels to fight their way through it to open water. But not without a price. All of the ships had been battered, especially the *Chance*, which suffered so much damage from the ice pack that her crew began to have serious doubts as to whether they could keep her afloat.

Ironically, the frightening experience that the men of the *Arctic, Lagoda, Daniel Webster, Midas, Chance, Europa,* and *Progress* had gone through was one of the few strokes of good luck that the whalers in the stricken fleet had received. It was while the seven vessels were struggling to free themselves from the ice that Captain Fraser had spotted them and had told them of the fleet's need of rescue. Had the seven vessels not been trapped so close to shore, they would have been farther out to sea, and Fraser, in all probability, would not have been able to make contact with them.

Once the seven vessels escaped their icy imprisonment, their troubles were not over. Almost as soon as they broke out of the ice pack, the weather turned even poorer, bringing with it rain, fog, and increasingly heavy seas. The huge chains that held the anchors about the *Midas* and the *Progress* were snapped in two, sending the enormous anchors to the bottom. The other ships were struggling mightily to hold their positions. The rescue of 1,219 fellow whalemen to which they were committed had now become an even more desperate race with time.

But just as the captains of the rescue vessels were beginning to think that perhaps they would have to sail away in order to protect their own ships and crews and were also beginning to lose hope that the multitude of stricken whalers would ever appear, the lookouts spotted an incredible sight. Scores of whaleboats were rounding Icy Cape. Inside each of the jam-packed boats, bobbing perilously up and down in the angry sea, men, women, and children were struggling to stay aboard. The rowers were battling desperately to keep their vessels moving forward. Meantime, each of the seven whaleships became a beehive of activity. The rescue attempt was about to begin.

Even in the best weather, the waters surrounding Icy Cape were treacherous for a heavy sailing vessel, let alone a light whaleboat. But the boats had arrived when the seas were particularly turbulent. To make matters worse, an enormous mass of newly formed ice protruded far out from the shore, making the journey around the point four times as long and considerably more dangerous.

One of the captains would later describe what happened next:

> *On the second day out, the boats reached [Icy Cape] and there spied the refuge-vessels lying five miles out from shore and behind a tongue of ice that stretched like a great peninsula ten miles farther down the coast, and around to the point of which the weary crews were obliged to pull.... The weather here was very bad, the wind blowing fresh from the southwest, causing a sea that threatened the little craft with annihilation. Still the hazardous journey had to be performed, and there was no time to be lost in setting about it.*
>
> *All submitted to this new danger ... and the little boats started on their almost hopeless voyage, even the women and children smothering their apprehensions as best they could. On the voyage along the inside of the [cape] everything went moderately well; but*

on rounding it, they encountered the full force of a tremendous southwest gale and a sea that would have made the stoutest ship tremble. In this fearful sea the whaleboats were tossed about like pieces of cork. They shipped quantities of water from every wave which struck them, requiring the utmost diligence of all hands to keep them afloat.

The captain was right. Getting to the rescue ships certainly required diligence. But it also required courage, strength, and all the years of seafaring experience that the men in the whaleboats possessed. Tossed by the towering seas, many of the boats spun around and had

---

This was the scene as the whaleboats, with men straining at the oars, attempted to make their way through the stormy ocean to the rescue ships.

to be brought back under control. In several of the boats, rowers had their oars broken by angry waves. Through it all, everyone was aware that managing to stay aboard, no matter how rough the seas, was absolutely essential. No one would be able to survive even a brief dunking in the freezing ocean.

It became clear also that if they were to make it to the ships, every provision and every personal treasure they had managed to get into the whaleboats would have to be tossed overboard to make the rowing easier. "I had to throw my bomb gun, a box of lances, [a] musket and lots of ammunition and several other things overboard [including]... Eskimo garments," Captain Nathaniel Ransom of the *John Wells* would later write. Lightening the load certainly helped, but, above all, it was the extra reserve that the rowers in most of the whaleboats somehow managed to find that enabled them to bring their small craft so close to the rescue vessels that they were hurled against the ships by the pounding waves. Some were damaged so badly that it seemed certain they would sink before those aboard could climb up the rope ladders that had been lowered to them.

Without hesitation, the captains and the crews of the rescue vessels then took over. Fortunately for the people in the boats, all of the captains of the rescue ships were seasoned mariners, used to dealing with crises at sea. Most had survived their own harrowing maritime experiences. Now bringing all their experience to bear, the captains of the seven whaleships raced from one side of their vessels to the other, shouting orders as they expertly directed the rescue operations.

The crewmen on each of the whaleships acted heroically as well. Some even risked their own lives by jumping into the stricken whaleboats and helping their occupants climb aboard the ships.

Not all the whaleboats, however, once having made it around the cape, were able to reach the ships. Once again, the captains of the rescue vessels sprang into action. As soon as they had taken aboard all of those in the boats alongside them, they began sailing their ships back and forth, dodging ice floes as their crews assisted those in the helplessly bobbing boats onto the ships. Even the *Chance*, more perilously in danger of foundering than ever, joined in this phase of the rescue.

As soon as the rescued whalemen were safely aboard the ships, they went belowdecks to dry out — but not before pausing to look back at another sad sight. William Fish Williams would later write that the *Progress*, which had rescued him and his family, "was pitching into the heavy seas that were running in a way that would make you wonder how we would get the men aboard, let alone the [women and] children. . . . As fast as the boats were unloaded they were cast adrift, to be destroyed against the ice pack a short distance [away] where the waves were breaking masthead high."

It had to be done. There was simply no room in the already overcrowded rescue vessels for the whaleboats. But, necessary as it was, it was difficult for all to see. As one newspaper would later report, the casting away of the whaleboats "was a tragedy second only to the first abandonment; these scores of graceful whaleboats, built with pride, and even with love, afloat empty for the first and last time, hastening down the wind to disaster, destined within minutes to become splinters on a barren beach. It was nothing for a boatman to watch."

What the boatmen could be eternally grateful for, however, was that, less than twenty-four hours after the first of these whaleboats had rounded Icy Cape, every person had been saved and had boarded one of the seven rescue vessels, which were now packed far beyond the capacity that their builders had ever envisioned. "On the *Progress*," William Fish Williams would write, "there were [more than 220] officers and men besides three ladies, and four children, one a baby in arms. Captain Dowden gave up his cabin and stateroom to the three captains with families. I have forgotten just how the three ladies and the younger children disposed of themselves in the stateroom, but in the after cabin we just managed to fit in by putting one man on the transom and two men and myself on the floor, but we were all very thankful for what we had. The other captains and officers divided quarters in the forward cabin, and rough berths were put up between decks for the sailors and boatsteerers, so that finally everybody was provided for except Captain Dowden, and I never did know where he managed to get his sleep."

Captain William Kelley put it more simply. "There were not accommodations for more than forty men on board on any of these ships," he observed, "yet in addition to their own crews they had to divide up the [more than] 1,200 of us."

Ahead lay the voyage to Honolulu, the nearest major port to which to deliver the rescued whalers. Overburdened as the ships were, it would be a long and arduous journey. But every person on each of the vessels, the rescuers and the rescued alike, knew that nothing short of a miracle had taken place. Twelve hundred and nineteen people who had come so close to perishing had been saved — and without a single loss of life.

On November 22, the last of the rescue vessels, the battered *Chance*, docked safely in Honolulu. For the men of the whaling fleet and their families it was a joyous occasion. But it would always be tempered by the fact that of the thirty-nine proud whaleships that had left Honolulu less than a year before, only seven had returned.

And the story was not over, for a big question still remained. Four of the whaleships had been destroyed by ice before the other twenty-eight vessels had been left behind. What had happened to the twenty-eight abandoned ships?

RIGHT: Soon after being saved by the *Progress*'s Captain James Dowden, seven of the rescued masters, including Thomas Williams, wrote a testimonial to Dowden, letting him and the world know that his actions would "never be forgotten."

TESTIMONIAL TO

Capt. James Dowden

A Copy of the Original now at Washington, D.C.

On Board Bark Progress, Oct. 23, 1871.

Capt. James Dowden,
        Master Bark Progress.

Dear Sir:

Allow us to thank you sincerely for your kindness, your trouble, and expense in transporting ourselves, our officers and crew from the Arctic Ocean to Honolulu.

We wish we were able to make you some compensation for the great pecuniary loss you have caused to be made to your own officers and crew, but such cannot be our pleasure.

Rest assured that your humane and generous conduct in rescuing one hundred and eighty-eight souls from suffering and death will never be forgotten. We should rejoice to learn that our government, whose gratitude you deservedly merit, had made you ample compensation for your loss.

Truly your friends,

Henry Pease, Jr.,	Master Ship	Champion,
Lewis Williams,	"	B'k Fanny,
B. D. Whitney,	"	" Wm. Rotch,
E. Everett Smith,	"	Carlotta,
T. D. Williams,	"	Monticello,
James H. Knowles,	"	Geo. Howland,
D. S. Redfield,	"	Brig Victoria.

CHAPTER SIX

Return to Point Belcher

TO A MARINER, there is nothing quite as sad as the sight of a once-proud ship lying in ruins, its days of glory only a memory.

— *Edward Rozwenc,* In Search of America, *1976*

What indeed had happened to the twenty-eight whaleships since they were left behind in the ice? It was a question that every one of the abandoned fleet's captains, now that they were safely out of the Arctic, could not help thinking about, none more so than Captain Thomas Williams.

From the moment that he and his family landed back in Honolulu and once again expressed their gratitude to the *Progress*'s Captain Dowden and his crew for having rescued them, Williams could not drive the thought of the abandoned ships out of his mind. Aside from the treasured ships themselves, he wondered, what had happened to the tons of whalebone and the thousands of barrels of oil that were stored in the vessels' holds and on their decks? And what about the *Monticello*, the ship that had been home to the Williams family for more than a year, the vessel that, as its captain, he had been entrusted to keep safely out of harm's way?

Williams's family hoped that eventually he would be able to put these agonizing questions aside. But just when it appeared that this might be the case, a report from a remote weather station located near Point Belcher was handed to the captain. According to the report, less than two weeks after the fleet was abandoned, at the very time that the jam-packed rescue vessels were heading back to Honolulu, yet another major Arctic weather event had taken place. Suddenly the strong wind shift that those who had been locked in the ice had fruitlessly prayed for had arrived, bringing with it a breakup of those types of ice packs that had imprisoned the fleet.

For Williams and most of the other captains, it was a maddening revelation. If the report was true, it meant that if the masters had delayed their decision to abandon the ships by just two weeks, perhaps the vessels could have been saved and perhaps 1,219 people would have been spared the most terrifying experience of their lives. To their credit, most of the captains, including Williams, knew that this was really useless speculation. They had made their decision to leave the ships at a time when there was no doubt in their minds that to delay any further meant losing their one slim opportunity for survival. Besides, they had no way of knowing if the report was in any way accurate.

But what if it was? Did that mean that some of the ships and their precious cargo might still be intact? Could the bone and oil be salvaged? Could the ships be sailed back to port? Now haunted more than ever, Thomas Williams knew what he had to do. He would outfit a vessel, man it with as many experienced whalemen as he could muster, and in the spring he would return to the site of the disaster. At the least, he thought, he would satisfy his burning curiosity as to what had happened to the fleet. At best, he would be able to arrange for a historic salvage operation.

Throughout 1871's long winter months, Williams made his preparations. He was pleased when the owners of the whaleship *Florence*, docked in San Francisco, agreed to lease him their vessel for his voyage. He was encouraged by the fact that he had been able to recruit a full crew for the upcoming journey, and was particularly pleased that his son Stancel had volunteered to join him on the trip.

By late April all was in readiness. As they set sail out of San Francisco Harbor, Williams and his crew were aware that they were embarking on a voyage much different from that any other whalemen headed for the Arctic had ever taken. Their ship was not loaded with whaling gear. There were no lookouts aloft keeping a watchful eye out for the sight of bowheads. They had only one mission in mind: to find the abandoned fleet and save whatever they could.

Six weeks later, the *Florida* entered the approaches to Point Belcher. The long trip had been without incident and, as they neared the area where the disaster had taken place, they were hoping to make a wonderful discovery. They made a discovery, all right — but it was far from wonderful. As they came upon the exact site of the abandonment, they encountered a scene unlike few other mariners had probably ever witnessed. Thirty-one of what had once been some of the finest whaling ships ever built lay in various states of destruction. Some, like the *Seneca*, had been carried up the coast by ice, winds, and tides and had been torn apart. Others, like the *Thomas Dickinson*, protruded bow or stern up from offshore banks, their holds caved in, their masts completely gone. Still others, including Henry Pease's *Champion*, the vessel on which the captains had made the decision to abandon the ships, lay in ruins along the shore. Many other vessels of the once-proud fleet had either been carried away by the ice or totally crushed.

It was a devastating sight. And for Thomas Williams it soon became even more depressing. As he and Stancel gazed out in shock, they suddenly spied yet another of the destroyed ships, submerged so deep in the water that only a portion of its bow protruded above the surface. But that portion was revealing enough. It was covered with the distinctive heavy iron plating that Williams had had placed all along the *Monticello*'s hull to protect it from the Arctic ice. Since the *Monticello* was the only ship in the fleet that had such a covering, Williams knew he had found his vessel. And it was a total loss.

Recovering from the shock of what had happened to the ship that he, his wife, and his children had boarded so confidently a year ago, Williams ordered his helmsmen to continue sailing from one wrecked vessel to another. As they looked out, they suddenly became dumbfounded. To their amazement, they discovered that several of the vessels had not been crushed by ice; they had been destroyed by fire. How, in this land of ice and snow, could that have happened? The answer was even more startling than the sight of the burned-out ships. After speaking with some of the hardy residents of the area, who had gathered on the shore, Williams and his men learned that the charred vessels had been deliberately set afire by Eskimos.

The whalemen were told that as the members of the icebound fleet had left their ships and taken to the open whaleboats, they had been observed by the natives. Soon it became clear to the Eskimos that no one would be returning to the vessels. To the natives, always hard pressed to sustain themselves in their barren land, the ships represented a treasure trove almost beyond belief. Aboard the ships, the Eskimos knew, were tons of provisions, including food and clothing that had, by necessity, been left behind. There was also the millions of dollars' worth of whalebone and oil.

Aside from all these treasures, there was all that canvas and wood, which could be used to build dwellings, all those ropes, and all the various types of cutting instruments and other tools. These were materials that the Eskimos could never have dreamed of owning, materials that would make their lives easier and richer than they had ever known.

By this time, the water between the land and the ships had become frozen solid. The natives simply walked to the vessels and, with the aid of sleds and dogs, hauled their booty away. For the better part of a week, working feverishly before new storms destroyed the ships, they removed everything they could.

Among the items that had been left behind in the captain's quarters on several of the vessels were the chests that contained the ship's medicine bottles. Already giddy over their newfound riches, many of the natives, thinking that the bottles contained pure liquor, not medicine, began downing the contents. Some drank so much that they became violently ill. A few of them died. Some of the remaining Eskimos, believing either that evil spirits had caused the calamity or that the white men had deliberately left the bottles behind to make whoever found them fatally sick, angrily set fire to the vessels and burned them down to the waterline.

After examining the remains of all the ships that had been destroyed and while searching the area for other vestiges of the ill-fated fleet, Williams and his men encountered yet another extraordinary sight. As they sailed into one of the area's inlets, they suddenly came upon another ship. It was the *Minerva*, standing tall and straight, and in as excellent a condition as she had been on the day she was abandoned.

Once again, the whalemen could only ask themselves, "How could this have happened?" How could this one vessel escape the ravages that had been heaped upon the other thirty-one ships and survive the Arctic winter in such perfect condition that it was ready to be sailed away in search of new whales and new adventures?

It was, as Williams and his crew later reported when they returned home, truly a miracle, but it was not the only one. The *Minerva* was not the only member of the 1871 fleet that had survived one of the worst winters in Arctic history. There was a human survivor as well and, in many ways, his was the most remarkable story of all.

After finding the *Minerva*, the whalemen continued exploring a wide area, searching for further remains of the 1871 fleet. They expected to find other wreckage, other bits and pieces of the ships that had been torn apart. What they never could have imagined was that suddenly a lone figure would appear, seemingly out of nowhere, walking toward them across the ice floes, shouting out to them for help. As he came closer it became clear that he was not an Eskimo but an American. Once taken aboard Williams's ship, the story he told was one of the most extraordinary tales that any of the crew had ever heard.

He was, he related, a member of the 1871 fleet. When the decision had been made to abandon the ships, he had come up with what he believed was an ingenious plan, one that would make him rich. On the day that everyone else left the ships and headed down the narrow channel in search of rescue, he stole away from his vessel, made his way across the ice to land, and hid. When the last whaleboat disappeared from view, he returned to one of the ships to begin living out his plan.

It was a simple scheme. He would do whatever it took to survive the Arctic winter, and in the spring when whalers returned to the region, he would, under salvage law, lay claim to all the bone, oil, and other possessions on the ships and become instantly wealthy. Was he crazy? Perhaps, but maybe not. Although the captains had correctly determined that there was not nearly enough food aboard the 1871 fleet to feed the more than

Jamie McKenzie made his first whaling voyage in 1853 when he was fourteen. By the age of twenty-three he had risen to the rank of first mate. Less than two years later, however, he was washed overboard in a storm and lost at sea.

Logbooks

———— ◎ ————

MUCH OF WHAT WE KNOW about how whaling was
carried out, what life was like aboard a whaling ship, and
about the countless adventures and exploits of those
who went whaling comes from the logbooks commonly
kept by either the captain or the first mate on each
vessel. Because they were written on the scene by those
who were either directly involved or eyewitness to what
took place, logs often provide us with the most accurate
accounts of what whaling was all about.

Written by men who for the most part felt that log
keeping was a tedious though necessary task, most log
entries were brief. A typical entry, for example, might
read, "Spotted seven whales. Gave chase. One whaleboat

stove in. Three whales taken. So ends the day."

In addition to the written accounts, it was not uncommon for logbook entries to be accompanied by colorful drawings. Some of these illustrations depicted spirited whaling activities. Most, however, were simple depictions of whales drawn to provide a record of how many barrels of oil or how many pounds of bone had been garnered in a specific day.

Those in which a whale was drawn vertically with its head facing downward indicated that the whale had been chased but escaped. A whale drawn broadside revealed that the whale had been captured. The number placed inside the drawing of the whale indicated how many barrels of oil or how many pounds of bone had been extracted from that particular creature.

twelve hundred people, there certainly was far more than enough to sustain one person indefinitely. He had his choice of vessels on which to live and, if he chose wisely, he thought he could move from ship to ship, depending upon the condition each was in at the time. And he understood enough about maritime law to know that, according to tradition, once a ship was abandoned, it and everything aboard it became the property of anyone who found and laid claim to it.

Actually, he told the whalers, he had begun by living ashore among a group of what he thought to be friendly Eskimos. After a while, however, most of the men in the group turned against the white outsider. "They threatened to kill me," he told the whalemen, "but the women saved me and afterward the old chief took care of me." Later on, when he became fearful that the women and the chief could no longer guarantee his safety, he moved back to the ships.

The vessel upon which he chose to ride out most of the winter was the *Massachusetts*, and it was aboard her that he became eyewitness to the destruction of the fleet. "Of all the butting and smashing I ever saw," he stated, "the [worst] was among those ships, driving into each other."

The man ended his story by telling Williams and his men that he had walked five miles across the ice to reach them, that all he had left from the riches he'd hoped to obtain were the clothes on his back, and that he was "pretty well used up." "A hundred and fifty thousand dollars," he stated, "would not tempt me to try another winter in the Arctic."

After hearing the astounding story, Williams sailed the *Florida* back to the *Minerva*. Then he put into motion a plan that had been forming in his mind since the very moment he had discovered the one surviving ship. He would, he told himself, salvage whatever bone and barrels of oil he could find in the fleet's wreckage, would transfer half of his crew to the *Minerva*, and would have his son Stancel sail the vessel and its cargo back to San Francisco.

One can only imagine the excitement that was caused when, in the fall of 1872, the *Minerva*, under full sail, appeared in San Francisco Harbor. By this time, news of the greatest disaster in whaling history had made headlines throughout the world. The unannounced appearance of the ship that had miraculously survived was an inspiration to whalemen everywhere.

For Thomas Williams, it was a time of deeply mixed

emotions. He had been devastated by the wreckage of the great whaling fleet. He knew that he would never forget the sight of the *Monticello* lying submerged beneath the sea. But he had done what he had set out to do. He had removed all doubt about the fate of the fleet. And he had brought the *Minerva* home.

CHAPTER SEVEN

End of an Era

COMPARABLE ONLY to the prairie schooner, the whaleship will always remain an American epic symbol.

— President Franklin D. Roosevelt, 1934

The name of the man who stayed behind has been lost to history. It is unfortunate, since he was the last player in the adventure that took place in the Arctic in 1871. It was a drama that, in many ways, signaled the beginning of the demise of the days of men in canvas-laden vessels sailing the world in search of whales. But it was a slow death.

Well into the twentieth century, whaleships, although in increasingly diminishing numbers, continued to pursue whales — whose numbers were also decreasing. And, despite what had happened to the 1871 fleet, some captains still challenged the Arctic waters.

Among them was Leander Owen, whose vessel, the *Contest*, had been one of the casualties of the 1871 disaster. Despite having suffered serious eye damage caused by snow blindness during the journey toward rescue at Icy Cape, Owen took several other ships in search of bowhead.

He was not alone. In 1876 a fleet of twenty whaleships sailed into the Arctic. Within days, twelve of the vessels were crushed by ice. Ironically, the captain of the ship that rescued the survivors of the crushed and sinking vessels was D. R. Fraser, the captain of the ill-fated *Florida* of the 1871 whaling fleet and the same man who had arguably become the greatest hero of the 1871 disaster by making the first treacherous journey down the narrow ice-filled channel and establishing contact with the rescue ships. Among the other whaleships destroyed in the 1876 catastrophe was the *Montenegro*, whose captain, William Kelley, had also lost his ship, the *Gay Head*, in the 1871 abandonment of the fleet.

Yet another victim of the 1876 disaster was the *Clara Bell*. Its captain was none other than Thomas Williams, who only four years earlier had returned to Point Belcher to discover what had happened to the ships left behind in 1871. Fortunately for Williams and his crew, the *Florence*, captained by Williams's brother Lewis, was close by when the *Clara Bell* went down, and Lewis and his crew were able to rescue his brother and his men.

The courage displayed by those who braved the dangers of hunting the greatest creatures on Earth has become one of whaling's most enduring legacies.

Why, one might ask, would such captains as D. R. Fraser and William Kelley return to the Arctic after having come so close to losing their lives and those of their crews in 1871? The answer is simple. These were men who had the sea and the love of adventure in their blood, men who had spent almost their entire lives aboard ships in search of whales.

Thomas Williams and his family serve as prime examples. Only two years after suffering through the 1871 disaster and then returning to Point Belcher, Williams took command of another vessel, and between 1873 and late 1875 made three successful whaling trips. Just as he had been undeterred by his 1871 experience, he was similarly unaffected by the 1876 disaster. In 1879 he returned once again to the Arctic, as captain of the whaleship *Francis Palmer*.

Williams's son Stancel, born on a whaleship, obviously inherited his father's passion for whaling. After sailing the *Minerva*, the one survivor of the 1871 fleet, back to port, he tried his hand at several businesses. But the call of the sea was too great. In 1889 he took command of his father's old ship the *Francis Palmer*, and for the next five years captained the vessel in pursuit of whales. Only the fact that on one of these voyages he was struck by a bomb lance, causing him to have to be fitted with a wooden leg, kept him from spending the rest of his life chasing whales.

Thomas Williams's brother Lewis, who had lost his ship *Fanny* in the ice in 1871 and who had rescued Thomas in the 1876 disaster, also could not get whaling out of his blood. After delivering Thomas and his crew safely back to port, Lewis immediately took another ship to the Arctic. The following year he sailed again to the region, where he and his crew had to be rescued when their vessel became yet another victim of an ice floe.

Remarkably, even this latest disaster did not faze Lewis Williams. For the next twenty-seven years he made his mark as one of the last of the whaling captains of the Age of Sail by taking three different whaleships — the *Hidalgo*, the *Andrew Hicks*, and the *California* — on a series of journeys in waters throughout the world.

Thomas Williams's youngest son, William Fish Williams, who had written so eloquently about the abandonment of his father's vessel in 1871, also returned to whaling. In 1874, only fifteen years old, he once again sailed on a whaleship commanded by his father. But this time he served in a much loftier position than cabin boy. He would never forget the moment that his father

Whalers of Color

──── ◉ ────

OVER THE YEARS, almost all the whalemen portrayed in motion pictures, novels, and television dramas have been white. It is a false representation. From the very beginning, men and women of color played a major, and sometimes predominant, role in the whaling industry.

The earliest whaleships commonly carried crews made up of white men and boys from New England, Native Americans from the Massachusetts island of Martha's Vineyard, and African Americans from many parts of the country. Beginning in the 1850s, as whaling became a major endeavor, whaleships, after leaving New Bedford or other eastern seaboard ports, stopped off at the Cape Verde Islands, where they would recruit as many as half of their crewmen. From that time on, Portuguese-speaking Cape Verdean Creoles, along with African Americans, became among the most numerous of whalemen.

African American contributions to whaling went well beyond the black whalemen themselves. Lewis Temple, for example, revolutionized the entire industry by inventing the toggle harpoon. Paul Cuffe became one of the nation's wealthiest citizens through the many whaleships his company built and the whaling vessels he owned and captained. African Americans connected with whaling also included some of America's most historic figures. Crispus Attucks, the first Colonial hero of the American Revolution, spent more than a decade as a whaleman before sacrificing his life at the Boston Massacre. After escaping from slavery, African American leader Frederick Douglass found refuge by working on New Bedford's whaling docks.

As whaling declined, men of color found even more opportunities. By 1900, many whaleships were owned, captained, and entirely manned by African Americans and Cape Verdeans.

decided which of the men under his command would serve as the boatsteerers (or stroke oars, as they were also called) of the ship's four whaleboat crews. "After my father had picked two men," Williams would later write, "and it came his turn to choose another, he turned to me and said, 'I will take my boy for the stroke oar of my boat.'

Survivors of the 1876 disaster await rescue after suffering through an Arctic tragedy that added a punctuation mark to the end of the glory days of whaling.

I had no intimation of this decision but nothing could have given me more pleasure and the event will always remain as one of the proudest moments of my life. I was fifteen years old and strong and I knew how to row."

William Fish Williams did himself and his father proud on the voyage and harpooned several whales. But unlike his father, his brother Stancel, or his uncle Lewis, he did not want to spend his life at sea. When his ship returned to its home port of New Bedford, he gave up whaling forever and went off to college, where he earned an engineering degree. He then began a fifty-four-year career of public service, starting in New Bedford, where he became the city's chief engineer. While in that position he designed the bridge that linked New Bedford to the neighboring whaling port of Fairhaven. Later he was appointed engineer of the Harbor and Land Commission of the state of Massachusetts, where, among other notable accomplishments, he took charge of building the Cape Cod Canal.

Stancel and William Fish Williams's sister, Mary, had also been born on a whaleship and had also been rescued off Icy Cape. Like her brothers, whaling was in her blood, and in 1897 she entered into a life that immersed her in the whaling industry. In that year in New Bedford she married Edgar Lewis, who owned a large fleet of whaleships. By this time New Bedford had become the whalebone center of the world, and Edgar Lewis had become known as the Whalebone King. The warehouses that Edgar and Mary owned were constantly filled with more than 100,000 pounds of whalebone, which was sold to high-priced dress and corset makers in New York and Paris.

Twice every year, Mary traveled with her husband to San Francisco, where they oversaw the fitting out of their many whaling vessels bound for the Arctic. In an age when most people believed that "a woman's place was in the home," Mary Williams Lewis turned out to have the most profound influence on whaling of all the members of her remarkable whaling family.

Not all those who returned to the sea despite their 1871 Arctic experiences went back to whaling. Captain Horace Newbury, for example, had had enough of both the Arctic and chasing the whale. But he too became restless on land. In the late 1870s, he served first as a mate and then as the captain of a merchant trading vessel. In 1885, after being at sea for more than thirty-two years, he finally retired and bought a farm. But the lure of the oceans was still too strong and, in the 1890s, he bought and skippered a fishing schooner, which he operated until his death in 1906.

Charles Allen, the captain who had been so eager to return to the Arctic in hope of once again coming home with a record-breaking catch, also gave up whaling. Those who knew him said that he did so out of sheer disappointment. For in the months before the ice set in, Allen had actually accomplished his goal. The bone and oil that he was forced to leave behind aboard the *J. D. Thomson* was actually greater in quantity and value than his previous record-breaking haul.

But even the disappointed Allen could not escape the call of the sea. In the late 1870s he entered the merchant marine as the captain of his own vessel, the *Sarah E. Allen*, named after his wife. In 1893, this talented whaleman, who had survived the greatest disaster in whaling history, lost his life when the *Sarah E. Allen* was torn apart at sea by a sudden and vicious storm.

The memory of the 1871 events was kept alive not only by the continued seafaring activities of several of the fleet's captains, but by the continued presence of some of the ships that had survived the disaster. The

Minerva, the one vessel that had miraculously survived the abandonment and the Arctic winter, made at least two more successful whaling voyages.

The *Lagoda*, whose heroic crew had played such an important role in the rescue of the men, women, and children of the whaling fleet, had a more unusual post-1871 history. Realizing that the glory days of whaling were coming to an end, the *Lagoda*'s owner sold the vessel to a company that used the ship to haul coal for fueling steamships docked in Yokohama, Japan. In 1899, the *Lagoda* was struck by a fire and destroyed off the Japanese coast. How ironic it was that this vessel that had for so long been a living symbol of the era of sail-driven craft had spent its last years serving the steam-driven vessels that brought an end to the Age of Sail. Today, a full half-scale model of the *Lagoda* stands in the New Bedford Whaling Museum, a vivid reminder of the ships, as well as the men and women, that made whaling one of the most unique, adventurous, and important enterprises in the nation's experience.

It was an adventure that remained forever fresh in the minds of all those who either took part in it or observed its triumphs and tragedies up close. Whaleman Charles Ashley spoke for all of those who mourned the passing of a way of life that would never come again. "As for [whale oil]," wrote Ashley, "I cannot smell it today without an attack of nostalgia: the faintest whiff and I see again the old New Bedford wharves, black with oil-soaked earth, rough-binned with seaweed-covered casks and fringed with long rows of . . . [square-rigged whaleships]. . . . Give me the smells of a . . . New Bedford wharf and all the refinements of the perfumer's art hold not a single charm."

It had indeed been a special time, one in which thousands of men and boys, along with the women and children who accompanied them, had lit the lamps of the world, had given people everywhere products that improved their lives, and had opened up the world as it had never been opened before. But despite the efforts of those like Leander Owen, D. R. Fraser, William Kelley, the Williams family, and scores of others to keep the enterprise alive, the Arctic disaster of 1871 put a punctuation mark on the decline of whaling as it had been known for more than one hundred years.

It had been an era not only of accomplishment but of extraordinary challenges as well. "Never in all of man's history," whaling historian Everett S. Allen would write, "has there been anything comparable to whaling in terms of what it demanded of those afloat who pursued it, or the vessels in which they sailed." There was no greater proof of this statement than the ordeal experienced by the more than 1,200 members of the 1871 fleet. It applied also to the captains and crewmen of the seven ships that rescued them. Several years after the rescue was accomplished, a special United States Congress report, written to inform the world of what had taken place in the frozen North, paid tribute to the sacrifices made by those who had saved so many lives:

These [seven] vessels had arrived on the whaling ground fully prepared to prosecute the business of whaling. The whales were plentiful in all directions. Suddenly ... a call is made upon them for [help] by 1,200 shipwrecked seamen. These men have no money to promise for the rescue. They are shut up in the Arctic seas with an Arctic winter before them and the sure result, if they are not rescued by these whaling vessels, is a slow lingering death, whether by starvation or cold.

The masters of these vessels have one alternative — on one hand, of turning their backs on these men and leaving them to die, while they go in the prosecution of their voyages and in making money for themselves, or, on the other, the sacrifice of their gains to rescue these shipwrecked sailors.

The choice was made without a moment's hesitation. The masters, with the full consent of the crews, decided at once to abandon their voyages, entirely regardless of self and without a murmur. They decided instantly to give up all hope of profit and all hope of reimbursing themselves for their expenses and to convey these men to a place of safety.

The same type of tribute could have been written about the 1,219 souls who displayed the courage necessary to get them through one of maritime history's greatest ordeals. All of those caught up in the 1871 Arctic disaster — rescuers and rescued alike — made their own special contribution. Trapped by circumstances beyond their control, or called upon to put their own personal gains aside, they each in their own way exhibited the bravery and the concern for their fellows that were the hallmarks of those who pitted themselves against both the sea and the largest creatures on Earth. In the end, it was this courage and this willingness to sacrifice that were perhaps whaling's greatest legacies of all.

RIGHT: This ca. 1920 photograph of the whaleship *Wanderer* embarking upon what would be one of the final whaling voyages out of New Bedford serves as a dramatic symbol of the end of what had been a truly remarkable era.

Further Reading

Collectively, the following books contain excellent accounts of every aspect of the whaling experience. Some were written years ago, during the great age of whaling, but are available in many libraries.

General Accounts

The following books deal with whaling in general and describe both the history of whaling and how whaling was carried out.

Murphy, Jim. *Gone A-Whaling*. New York: Clarion Books, 1998.

Shapiro, Irwin. *The Story of Yankee Whaling*. New York: American Heritage, 1959.

Starbuck, Alexander. *History of the American Whale Fishery*. Secaucus, NJ: Castle Books, 1989.

Verrill, A. Hyatt. *The Real Story of the Whaler*. New York: D. Appleton, 1923.

Firsthand Accounts

The following books are filled with spirited accounts of the authors' experiences during their whaling voyages.

Ashley, Clifford. *The Yankee Whaler*. Garden City, NY: Halcyon House, 1942.

Browne, J. Ross. *Etchings of a Whaling Cruise*. New York: Harper, 1846.

Cheever, Henry. *The Whale and His Captors*. New York: Harper, 1853.

Davis, William. *Nimrod of the Sea*. North Quincy, MA: Christopher Publishing, 1972.

Haley, Nelson Cole. *Whale Hunt*. New York: Ives Washburn, 1948.

Whaling Captains

This book tells the stories and describes the adventures of more than a score of whaling captains.

Colby, Bernard. *For Oil and Buggy Whips*. Mystic, CT: Mystic Seaport Press, 1990.

African American Whalers

This book includes a description of the role of African Americans in the whaling industry.

Bolster, W. Jeffrey. *Black Jacks: African American Seamen in the Age of Sail*. Cambridge, MA: Harvard University Press, 1997.

A Whaling Family

The following book contains the reminiscences, logbook entries, and stories of Thomas and Eliza Williams and their children, all of whom spent years at sea on whaling vessels.

Williams, Harold, ed. *One Whaling Family*. Boston: Houghton Mifflin, 1964.

Arctic Disaster

This well-researched, highly readable book has become a standard for students of whaling and contains the first published account of the Arctic disaster of 1871.

Allen, Everett S. *Children of the Light*. Boston: Little, Brown, 1973.

Whaling Stories

These two books contain stories of dramatic incidents in whaling, including mutinies, desertions, and amazing encounters with whales.

Howland, Chester S. *Thar She Blows*. New York: Wilfred Funk, 1951.

Watson, Arthur. *The Long Harpoon*. New Bedford, MA: Reynolds Printing, 1929.

Whalecraft

This book describes how whales were pursued and how they were captured, with a special emphasis on the array of equipment used by the whalemen.

Giambarba, Paul. *Whales, Whaling, and Whalecraft*. Centerville, MA: Scrimshaw Press, 1967.

Glossary
OF WHALING TERMS

AFT: At, near, or toward the stern (rear) of a vessel.

ALOFT: Above the deck, in the rigging.

BLANKET PIECE: A long strip of blubber stripped from a whale.

BLOW: The cloud of moisture exhaled by whales when breathing out upon surfacing.

BLOWHOLE: A whale's nostril, located on top of its head. Bowhead whales have two blowholes; sperm whales have one.

BLUBBER: The thick, oily layer of fat immediately below the skin of a whale.

BOATHEADER: The man who steered the whaleboat toward a whale and who killed it with a lance after it was harpooned.

BOATSTEERER: The man who pulled the foremost oar in the whaleboat, harpooned the whale, and then manned the whaleboat's rudder.

BOW: The front end of a ship or boat.

CASE: The forehead of a sperm whale.

COOPER: The person who made the barrels or casks in which whale oil was stored on a whaleship.

CUTTING-IN: The process of removing blubber from a whale.

DECK: The "floor" of a ship.

FITTING OUT: The process of getting a ship ready for a whaling voyage.

FLUKES: The two lobes at the end of a whale's tail.

FLURRY: The final death struggle of a whale.

FORE: Near the front (or bow) of a vessel.

GAM: An exchange of visits at sea by the crews of two or more vessels.

GREEN HAND: A man or boy on his first whaling voyage.

HARPOON: The barbed iron instrument used to fasten on to a whale.

HOLD: The space belowdecks on a whaleship, where whale oil and bone were stored.

IRON: Another term for *harpoon*.

KEEL: A long timber running lengthwise down the center bottom of a ship.

KNOT: A unit of speed at sea, approximately 1.5 miles per hour.

LINE: The rope attached to a harpoon when fastened to a whale.

MAST: An upright pole for supporting sails and ropes.

MASTER: A whaling captain.

MATE: An officer of a ship.

MINCE: To cut into small pieces.

PORT: The left-hand side of a ship facing forward.

RIGGING: The distinctive arrangement of ropes, chains, and tackle used to control a ship's sails.

SCRIMSHAW: Decorative or useful objects made from the teeth of sperm whales or the bones of bowheads.

SKIPPER: A ship's captain.

STARBOARD: The right-hand side of a ship facing forward.

STERN: The rear of a ship.

TRY-POTS: The large iron kettles in which a whale's blubber was boiled to extract the oil.

TRYWORKS: The brick structure that held the try-pots.

YARDS: Horizontal poles that crossed the masts and supported the sails on a whaling vessel. The ends of these poles were called yardarms.

Acknowledgments

THE AUTHOR WISHES to thank Ken Wright, who once again recognized a story that needed to be told. Thanks are due also to Michael Lapides, Mary Jean Blasdale, and Michael Dyer of the New Bedford Whaling Museum for their much-appreciated aid and support. As usual, John Thornton and Carol Sandler provided valuable insight and support. A special nod goes to Kyle Gilmore, a young scholar-to-be who was the first to read and be excited about the manuscript. The author is particularly indebted to Paula Manzanero, both for her superior editing skills and her many contributions in shaping this book.

Art Credits

Index

in Arctic waters, 69–70
training of, 50–60
Gulf Stream, first chart of, 15

H

Haley, Nelson Cole, 17
Harpooners, 66–67
Harpoons, 53–57
  first to use, 56–57
  manufacture of, 57
Helen Mar, 13
  sinking of, 8–9
Henry Taber, 78, 82–83, 84, 100
Hibernia, 40–41, 46
Homes, Captain Joseph, 28–30
Honolulu Harbor, 26–27, 48
  voyage of rescued whalers to, 117–118

I

Ice fields, 9–12
  in Arctic waters, 68, 71–72
  dangers of, 12–25
  escape from, 90–119
Ice packs, 73–76, 78–88
Icy Cape, 85–86, 87
  whaleboats icebound in, 90–118
Inuits, 56

J

J. D. Thomson, 36, 145
Jernagen, Mrs. Nathaniel, 44–45
John Wells, 114

K

Kelley, Captain William, 84–85, 86, 117, 136, 138, 147
Kohola, 86–87

L

Lagoda, 146
Lamp oil, 18–19, **20–21**
Lawrence, Mary, 44
Lewis, Edgar, 144
Lewis, Mary Williams, 144
Logbooks, 130–131
Lookouts, **88–89**

M

Mammoth, 16–17
Massachusetts, 76, 132
Mayhew, Captain, 45
Mayhew, Caroline, 45
McKenzie, Jamie, **129**
Melville, Herman, 33, 49–50
Midas, 109–110
Minerva, 127–128, 133, 138, 145–146
Moby Dick, 49–50
Montenegro, 136
Monticello, 37, 39, 43–46, 75–76, 121, 134
  remains of, 124–125

N

Nantucket sleigh ride, 54–55
Native American whalers, 140
Navigation, 28–30
New Bedford, Massachusetts, 27, 32–33, **38–39**, 143–144
New Bedford Whaling Museum, 146
Newbury, Captain Horace, 31–36, 77, 84–85, 100, 144–145
Northern Light, 22–23

O

Oil, whale, 18–19, 61–63
  boiling blubber down to, 69